GRAMMAR
Form and Function

1A

Workbook

Milada Broukal
Amy Parker

 McGraw-Hill

ESL23

Grammar Form and Function 1A Workbook

This book is printed on recycled, acid-free paper containing 10% postconsumer waste.

3 4 5 6 7 8 9 QPD 9 8 7 6 5

ISBN: 0-07-301197-5

Editorial director: Tina B. Carver
Executive editor: Erik Gundersen
Sr. developmental editor: Annie Sullivan
Editorial assistant: Kasey Williamson
Production manager: MaryRose Bollwage
Cover design: Preface, Inc.
Interior design: Preface, Inc.
Art: Eldon Doty, Preface, Inc.

Photo credits:
All photos are courtesy of Getty Images Royalty-Free Collection, except p.91 Buzz Aldrin. Page 91, view of Astronaut Edwin (Buzz) E. Aldrin Jr. in Lunar Module courtesy of NASA.

Mc Graw Hill **McGraw-Hill**

Contents

UNIT 3   THE SIMPLE PRESENT TENSE

UNIT 4   THE PRESENT PROGRESSIVE TENSE

UNIT 5   NOUNS AND PRONOUNS

UNIT 6   THE SIMPLE PAST TENSE

UNIT 7   THE PAST PROGRESSIVE TENSE

UNIT 1
THE PRESENT TENSE OF *BE*

1a Nouns: Singular

Student Book p. 2

1 Practice

Write *a* or *an* before the noun.

1. __*an*__ egg
2. _____ bird
3. _____ university
4. _____ orange
5. _____ horse

6. _____ hour
7. _____ flower
8. _____ boy
9. _____ cat
10. _____ teacher

2 Practice

Write *C* next to the phrase if *a* or *an* is correct. Write *I* if *a* or *an* is incorrect.

1. __*I*__ a elephant
2. __*C*__ an office
3. _____ a teacher
4. _____ a apple
5. _____ a man

6. _____ an hour
7. _____ a city
8. _____ an horse
9. _____ a book
10. _____ a uncle

1b Nouns: Plural

Student Book p. 3

3 Practice

Write the plural.

1. cat   __*cats*__
2. foot   _____
3. man   _____
4. baby   _____
5. life   _____

6. box   _____
7. dish   _____
8. woman   _____
9. child   _____
10. country _____

4 Practice

Circle the correct form of the noun.

1. two (bus / **buses**)
2. four (knifes / **knives**)
3. six (babys / **babies**)
4. three (womans / **women**)
5. ten (**watches** / watchs)
6. one (**tooth** / teeth)
7. nine (**sheep** / sheeps)

8. eight (childs / **children**)
9. five (**mice** / mouses)
10. two (mans / **men**)
11. three (**lives** / lifes)
12. ten (countrys / **countries**)
13. six (dish / **dishes**)
14. nine (**fish** / fishes)

1c Subject Pronouns

Student Book p. 5

5 Practice

Write *he, she, it,* or *they* under the photos.

1. _____

2. _____

3. _____

4. _____

5. _____

6 Practice

Write *he, she, it,* or *they* beside the word or phrase.

1. students _____
2. city _____
3. Maria _____
4. babies _____
5. Mr. Lee _____
6. Susan and Rose _____

7. male cat _____
8. book _____
9. man _____
10. Ms. Katz _____
11. girl _____
12. women _____

1d Subject Pronoun + Present Tense of *Be*

Student Book p. 8

7 Practice

Complete the sentences. Use *am, is,* or *are.*

1. You ___*are*___ from Egypt.
2. They _____ students.
3. I _____ hungry.
4. He _____ a teacher.
5. We _____ friends.

6. It _____ an egg.
7. Jack and Bob _____ from Canada.
8. The sandwich _____ good.
9. Junko _____ a student.
10. The house _____ white.

8 Practice

Complete the sentences with contractions of *be* and the pronouns in parentheses.

1. (I) ___*I'm*___ from Brazil.
2. (She) _____ a woman.
3. (You) _____ a student.
4. (We) _____ late.
5. (He) _____ a baby.

6. (It) _____ a car.
7. (They) _____ beautiful.
8. (You) _____ a doctor.
9. (I) _____ Chinese.
10. (It) _____ an umbrella.

1e Negative of *Be*

Student Book p. 10

9 Practice

Complete the sentences. Use the long form of the negative *(am not, is not, are not)*.

1. I _____*am not*_____ a teacher. I'm a student.

2. We _____ from Germany. We're from Switzerland.

3. They _____ 17 years old. They're 19 years old.

4. He _____ a boy. He's a man.

5. She _____ Italian. She's Brazilian.

6. You _____ a doctor. You're a teacher.

7. It _____ a lemon. It's an orange.

8. They _____ buses. They're cars.

9. It _____ a magazine. It's a newspaper.

10. I _____ Chilean. I'm American.

10 Practice

Use the chart to complete the sentences with *is/isn't* or *are/aren't*.

Name	Country	Age	Occupation
Maria Elena	Brazil	34	doctor
Ling Yi	China	21	student
Marco	Italy	32	teacher
Yu Jen	China	26	student

1. Maria Elena _____*isn't*_____ from Italy. She _____*is*_____ from Brazil.

2. Maria Elena _____ 34. She _____ 23.

3. Ling Yi and Yu Jen _____ from China. They _____ from Italy.

4. Ling Yi _____ a student. She _____ a doctor.

5. Marco _____ 32. He _____ a teacher.

6. Marco _____ from Italy. He _____ China.

7. Yu Jen _____ 28. He _____ 26.

8. Ling Yi and Yu Jen _____ students. They _____ teachers.

II Practice

Write _C_ next to the sentence if _be_ is correct. Write _I_ if _be_ is incorrect.

1. __C__ We're from Italy.

2. __I__ I isn't a teacher.

3. _____ Marie Elena are a doctor.

4. _____ The women isn't beautiful.

5. _____ They're students.

6. _____ She's Canadian.

7. _____ You is not 25.

8. _____ He aren't a boy.

9. _____ The umbrella is red.

10. _____ The country are big.

1f Be + Adjective

Student Book p. 12

I2 Practice

Complete the sentences with _is_ or _are_ and one of the following adjectives.

| cold | cute | hot | salty | soft | yellow |

1. The babies _____are cute_____.

2. The ocean _____.

3. Fire _____.

4. Winter _____.

5. The cats _____.

6. The sun _____.

I3 Practice

Complete the sentences with the affirmative or negative contraction of _be_ and one of the following adjectives.

| French | sad | shy | single |
| lazy | short | sick | young |

1. Rosemary is healthy. _She isn't sick_____.

2. Rosemary is hardworking. _____.

3. She isn't old. _____.

4. She's friendly. _____.

5. She isn't married. _____.

6. Rosemary isn't tall. _____.

7. Rosemary is happy. _____.

8. She isn't American. _____.

The Present Tense of _Be_

14 Practice

Complete the sentences about you, your family, and your friends. Use the following adjectives or your own and *'m/'m not* or *is/isn't*.

friendly	healthy	married	short	single
happy	heavy	old	shy	slim
hardworking	lazy	sad	sick	tall
				young

1. I *'m married* _____. I *'m not single* _____.

2. I _____. I _____.

3. I _____. I _____.

4. I _____. I _____.

5. I _____. I _____.

6. I _____. I _____.

7. I _____. I _____.

8. My best friend *is heavy* _____. He/She *isn't slim* _____.

9. My best friend _____. He/She _____.

10. My best friend _____. He/She _____.

11. My best friend _____. He/She _____.

12. My best friend _____. He/She _____.

15 Practice

Complete the sentences with the adjective for the country and the correct form of *be*. You may use contractions.

1. She's from England. (She) *She's English.* (OR) *She is English* .

2. Peg and Julie are from America. (They) _____.

3. Nelson is from Brazil. (He) _____.

4. Simone is from France. (She) _____.

5. Kasey and Thomas are from Canada. (They) _____.

6. Yucel is from Turkey. (He) _____.

7. Katherine is from Korea. (She) _____.

8. Yuhi and Daigo are from Japan. (They) _____.

1g Possessive Adjectives

Student Book p. 18

16 Practice

Complete the sentences with *my, your, his, her, our,* or *their*.

___My___ name is Marcella. I'm single. I have a sister. _____ name
₁ 2

is Johana. _____ sister is married. _____ husband's name is Jorge.
3 4

They have a house. _____ house is big. They have a little girl and a little
5

boy. _____ boy is four years old. _____ name is Alejandro.
6 7

_____ girl is two years old. _____ name is Gabriella. I have a
8 9

brother too. _____ name is Arturo. We have a mother and a father.
10

_____ parents live in Venezuela.
11

17 Practice

**Use the chart to complete the sentences about Johana, Arturo, their cousins, and you.
Use *his, her, their,* and *my*.**

	Johana	Arturo	Their cousins	You
Animal	cat	giraffe	elephant	*horse*
Class	science	history	English	
Color	green	red	blue	

1. ___Her___ favorite animal is the cat.

2. ___Their___ favorite color is blue.

3. _____ favorite class is history.

4. _____ favorite animal is the elephant.

5. _____ favorite color is green.

6. _____ favorite animal is the giraffe.

7. _____ favorite class is English.

8. _____ favorite class is science.

9. ___My___ favorite animal is the ___horse___.

10. _____ favorite sport is _____.

11. _____ favorite food is _____.

Student Book p. 20

18 Practice

Complete the sentences with *my, your, his, her, our,* or *their*.

1. I have a brother. He's _____*my*_____ brother.

2. They have a car. It's _____ car.

3. She has a baby. It's _____ baby.

4. You have a sister. She's _____ sister.

5. We have a house. It's _____ house.

6. My father has keys. They're _____ keys.

7. I have a cat. It's _____ cat.

8. She has chocolate. It's _____ chocolate.

9. You have a good class. It's _____ class.

10. David has a book. It's _____ book.

1h Demonstrative Adjectives

Student Book p. 20

19 Practice

Complete the sentences with *this, that, these,* or *those*.

1. _*This*_____ is my mouth.

2. _____ are my teeth.

3. _____ are my eyes.

4. _____ is my nose.

5. _____ are my ears.

6. _*That*_____ is my dog.

7. _____ are my shoes.

8. _____ is my bed.

9. _____ is my window.

10. _____ are my books.

20 Practice

Write C next to the sentence if *these, those, this,* or *that* is correct. Write *I* if *these, those, this,* or *that* is incorrect.

1. __C__ These are my books.

2. __I__ This are his brothers.

3. _____ Those are oranges.

4. _____ Are this your pens?

5. _____ Those are cute babies.

6. _____ That is a big car.

7. _____ These student is from Italy.

8. _____ Those man is a teacher.

9. _____ This is an office.

10. _____ That are elephants.

1i Yes/No Questions with *Be*

Student Book p. 22

21 Practice

Read the following information forms. Then complete the questions and answers about Sylvia and Kevin.

Name:	Sylvia Hernandez
Age:	31
Occupation:	Doctor
Nationality:	Mexican
Marital Status:	Single

Name:	Kevin Park
Age:	35
Occupation:	Teacher
Nationality:	Korean
Marital Status:	Divorced

1. _____ Is he _____ a doctor?   No, he isn't.

2. _____ young?   Yes, they are.

3. _____ Korean?   No, _____.

4. _____ Mexican?   Yes, _____.

5. _____ married?   No, _____.

6. _____ divorced?   Yes, _____.

7. _____ 31?   No, _____.

8. _____ 31?   Yes, _____.

22 Practice

Complete the questions and write the answers.

1. _Are they_ _____ apples?

   No, they're not. (OR) _No, they aren't_ .

   They're oranges _____.

2. _____ sweet?

   _____.

   _____.

3. _____ big?

   _____.

   _____.

4. _____ a man?

   _____.

   _____.

5. _____ a brunette?

   _____.

   _____.

6. _____ slim?

   _____.

   _____.

7. _____ a chair?

   _____.

   _____.

8. _____ rectangular?

   _____.

   _____.

9. _____ soft?

   _____.

   _____.

1j Questions with *What*, *Where*, and *Who*

Student Book p. 26

23 Practice

Match the questions with the answers.

Questions		Answers
_____	**1.** What's your name?	**a.** They are in Japan.
_____	**2.** Where are you from?	**b.** I'm from Tokyo.
_____	**3.** Who's that man?	**c.** She's my cousin.
_____	**4.** What is it?	**d.** He's my brother.
_____	**5.** Who's she?	**e.** My name is Naomi Honda.
_____	**6.** Where are they?	**f.** It's a photo.

24 Practice

Write questions with *who*, *what*, or *where*.

1. <u>What's your name</u> ? My name is Peter Wang.

2. _____ ? I'm from Singapore.

3. _____ ? It's a mountain.

4. _____ ? He's my father.

5. _____ ? She's my teacher.

6. _____ ? They're clouds.

7. _____ Joanne? She's at school.

8. _____ your parents? They're in Peru.

1k ◆ Prepositions of Place

Student Book p. 28

25 Practice

Complete the sentences with the prepositions *on*, *in front of*, *under*, or *behind*.

1. The apple is _____ *in front of* _____ the box.

2. The cat is _____ the box.

3. The box is _____ the cat.

4. The books are _____ the box.

5. The box is _____ the apple.

6. The box is _____ the books.

26 Practice

Complete the sentences with the prepositions *above, below, next to,* or *between*.

A	B	C	D	E	F	G	H	I	J	K	L	M
N	O	P	Q	R	S	T	U	V	W	X	Y	Z

1. W is _____ *next to* _____ X.   6. S is _____ F.

2. O is _____ N and P.   7. B is _____ C.

3. D is _____ E.   8. T is _____ S and U.

4. C is _____ P.   9. M is _____ Z.

5. I is _____ H and J.   10. V is _____ I.

SELF-TEST

A   Choose the best answer, A, B, C, or D, to complete the sentence. Mark your answer by darkening the oval with the same letter.

1. _____ are you from?

   A. Who   Ⓐ Ⓑ Ⓒ Ⓓ
   B. What
   C. Where
   D. Who're

2. _____ friendly.

   A. She're   Ⓐ Ⓑ Ⓒ Ⓓ
   B. She's
   C. She are
   D. Her

3. _____ from Brazil.

   A. I'm   Ⓐ Ⓑ Ⓒ Ⓓ
   B. She are
   C. My
   D. I

4. They have two _____.

   A. baby   Ⓐ Ⓑ Ⓒ Ⓓ
   B. babys
   C. child
   D. babies

5. _____ are flowers.

   A. Those   Ⓐ Ⓑ Ⓒ Ⓓ
   B. That
   C. This
   D. It

6. We're _____.

   A. a student   Ⓐ Ⓑ Ⓒ Ⓓ
   B. students
   C. student
   D. a students

7. You're _____.

   A. English   Ⓐ Ⓑ Ⓒ Ⓓ
   B. China
   C. Brazil
   D. Thailand

8. They _____ teachers.

   A. am not   Ⓐ Ⓑ Ⓒ Ⓓ
   B. is
   C. aren't
   D. isn't

9. The desk is _____ the window.

   A. next to   Ⓐ Ⓑ Ⓒ Ⓓ
   B. between
   C. from
   D. your

10. A: _____ that woman?
    B: That's my sister.

   A. Who   Ⓐ Ⓑ Ⓒ Ⓓ
   B. Where's
   C. What's
   D. Who's

B   **Find the underlined word or phrase, A, B, C, or D, that is incorrect. Mark your answer by darkening the oval with the same letter.**

1. I have two big foots.
   A   B   C   D

   Ⓐ Ⓑ Ⓒ Ⓓ

2. Sarah and I is not teachers.
   A   B C   D

   Ⓐ Ⓑ Ⓒ Ⓓ

3. She are not a student.
   A   B   C   D

   Ⓐ Ⓑ Ⓒ Ⓓ

4. These is my book.
   A   B C   D

   Ⓐ Ⓑ Ⓒ Ⓓ

5. A elephant is heavy.
   A   B   C   D

   Ⓐ Ⓑ Ⓒ Ⓓ

6. What are your name?
   A   B   C   D

   Ⓐ Ⓑ Ⓒ Ⓓ

7. What are you from?
   A   B   C   D

   Ⓐ Ⓑ Ⓒ Ⓓ

8. These teachers are not at Japan.
   A   B   C   D

   Ⓐ Ⓑ Ⓒ Ⓓ

9. Those women is not teachers.
   A   B   C   D

   Ⓐ Ⓑ Ⓒ Ⓓ

10. This car are expensive.
    A   B   C   D

   Ⓐ Ⓑ Ⓒ Ⓓ

UNIT 2 BE: IT, THERE, AND THE PAST TENSE OF BE

2a *It* to Talk about the Weather
Student Book p. 34

1 Practice
Look at the weather map. Then answer the questions.

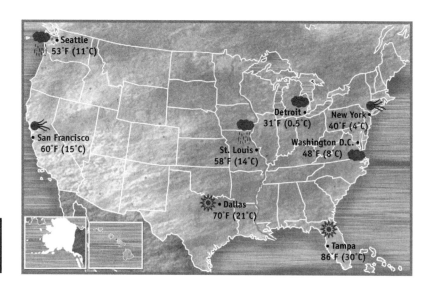

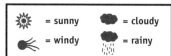

1. What's the weather like in Seattle? _____ *It's rainy* _____ .

2. Is it cool in Seattle today? _____ .

3. What's the temperature in New York? _____ .

4. What's the weather like in Dallas? _____ .

5. What's the temperature in Dallas? _____ .

6. How's the weather in San Francisco? _____ .

7. What's the temperature in San Francisco? _____ .

8. Is it hot or cold in Detroit today? _____ .

9. Is it sunny in Tampa? _____.

10. How's the weather in Tampa? _____.

11. Is it windy in Washington, D.C.? _____.

12. What's the weather like in Washington, D.C.? _____.

13. How's the weather in St. Louis? _____.

14. Is it sunny in St. Louis? _____.

15. What's the temperature in Detroit? _____.

2 Practice

Answer the questions.

1. Is it sunny today? _____

2. What's the weather like today? _____

3. What's the temperature today? _____

2b *It* to Tell Time
Student Book p. 36

3 Practice

Write sentences telling the times shown on the clocks.

1. _It's two o' clock_ . **2.** _____ **3.** _____

4. _____ **5.** _____ **6.** _____

7. _____   8. _____   9. _____

10. _____   11. _____   12. _____

4   Practice

Match the questions with the answers.

Questions

  _d___ **1.** What time is it?

_____ **2.** What day is it?

_____ **3.** What month is it?

_____ **4.** What's the date today?

_____ **5.** What year is it?

Answers

a. It's 2004.

b. It's April 6th.

c. It's April.

d. It's 9:15.

e. It's Saturday.

5   Practice

Answer the questions.

1. What time is it? _____ .

2. What month is it? _____ .

3. What year is it? _____ .

4. What day is it? _____ .

5. What's the date today? _____ .

2c Questions with *When, What Day,* and *What Time;* Prepositions of Time

Student Book p. 38

6 Practice

Complete the sentences with the prepositions of time *in, on, at,* or *from ... to.*

1. I was born _____*in*_____ September.

2. I was born _____ September 17, 1983.

3. My family moved to the United States _____ 1996.

4. I eat lunch _____ one o'clock.

5. My class is _____ 8:30 A.M.

6. My band practices _____ 8:30 P.M. _____ 11:30 P.M.

7. My band practices _____ Tuesday and Friday.

8. I work _____ Monday and Wednesday.

9. I go to work _____ the evening.

10. I cook dinner _____ night.

11. We study _____ 7:00 _____ 9:00.

12. I have a meeting with my teacher _____ November 23rd.

13. The appointment is _____ the afternoon.

14. It's _____ 2:15.

7 Practice

Write *C* next to the phrase if *in, on,* or *at* is correct. Write *I* if *in, on,* or *at* is incorrect.

___*I*___ **1.** in Tuesday   _____ **5.** on Thursday

___*C*___ **2.** at 2 o'clock   _____ **6.** in 3:30 P.M.

_____ **3.** on Sunday   _____ **7.** in the evening

_____ **4.** on July   _____ **8.** in December

8 Practice

Write answers to the questions.

April						
S	M	T	W	T	F	S
		April 1 Fool's Day	2	3	4	5
6	7	8	9	10	11	12
13	14	15	16	17	18	19
20	21	22	23 doctor 2:30	24	25	26
27 my birth-day	28	29	30			

1. When is April Fool's Day?

   _It's in April. It's on April 1st_____.

2. What day is April Fool's Day?

   _____.

3. When is my birthday?

   _____.

4. What day is my birthday?

   _____.

5. When is my doctor's appointment?

   _____.

6. What day is my doctor's appointment?

   _____.

May						
S	M	T	W	T	F	S
				1 May Day	2	3
4	5	6	7	8	9	10
11	12	13	14	15	16	17 Party 8:00
18	19	20	21	22	23 last class	24
25	26 Memorial Day	27	28	29	30	

7. When is May Day?

   _____.

8. What day is May Day?

   _____.

9. When is Memorial Day?

   _____.

10. What day is Memorial Day? _____.

11. When is the party? _____.

12. What day is the party? _____.

13. When is the last day of class? _____.

14. What day is the last day of class? _____.

Be: It, There, and the Past Tense of *Be*

2d Statements with *There + Be*

Student Book p. 41

9 **Practice**

Look at the office. Complete the sentences with *there is* or *there are*.

1. _There is_____ a desk in the office.

2. _____ two chairs in front of

   the desk.

3. _____ a computer on the desk.

4. _____ a phone next to the

   computer.

5. _____ windows in the office.

6. _____ a clock in the office.

7. _____ books on the chair.

10 **Practice**

Look at the bedroom and complete the sentences with *there's/there are* or *there isn't/there aren't*.

1. _There's_____ a computer in the room.

2. _There isn't_____ a backpack in the room.

3. _____ beds.

4. _____ a clock.

5. _____ any dishes.

6. _____ a television.

7. _____ a desk.

8. _____ any books.

9. _____ a window.

10. _____ any children.

11. _____ some glasses.

12. _____ a DVD player.

11 Practice

Write ten sentences about things that are and are not in your bedroom.

1. *There aren't any cats in my bedroom* .
2. _____ .
3. _____ .
4. _____ .
5. _____ .
6. _____ .
7. _____ .
8. _____ .
9. _____ .
10. _____ .

2e Questions with *There + Be*

Student Book p. 44

12 Practice

Read the advertisement for an apartment building. Then complete the questions and answers with *there is, there isn't, there are, there aren't, is there*, or *are there*.

Lakeside Apartments

There are 15 apartments in the building. An apartment has two bedrooms and one kitchen. There is a parking lot. You are next to three parks! There are four restaurants and one library near the building. There are three schools and one church, too. The bus takes you downtown in 15 minutes.

1. *Is there* a kitchen in the apartment?

   Yes, there is .

2. *Are there* any mountains near the apartments?

   _____ .

Be: It, There, and the Past Tense of Be

3. _____ any parks near the building?

_____.

4. _____ any schools?

_____.

5. _____ a train?

_____.

6. _____ a parking lot?

_____.

7. _____ a swimming pool?

_____.

8. _____ a library?

_____.

9. How many bedrooms _____ _are there_ _____ in the apartment?

_____.

10. How many restaurants _____?

_____.

11. How many churches _____?

_____.

12. How many schools _____?

_____.

13 Practice

Ask and answer the questions using *how many, are there, there is,* or *there are.*

1. _How many_ books _are there_ in your room?

There are nine books in my room .

2. _____ clocks _____ in your room?

_____.

3. _____ desks _____ in your room?

_____.

22

Unit 2

4. _____ windows _____ in your room?

_____ .

5. _____ telephones _____ in your room?

_____ .

6. _____ cats _____ in your room?

_____ .

7. _____ shoes _____ in your room?

_____ .

8. _____ beds _____ in your room?

_____ .

14 ## Practice

Write questions with *how many* using the prompts. Then write the answers.

1. letters/the alphabet   *How many letters are there in the alphabet* ?

   There are 26   .

2. months/a year   _____ ?

   _____ .

3. days/April   _____ ?

   _____ .

4. desks/your classroom   _____ ?

   _____ .

5. meters/a kilometer   _____ ?

   _____ .

6. milligrams/a gram   _____ ?

   _____ .

7. pages/this unit   _____ ?

   _____ .

8. exercises/this page   _____ ?

   _____ .

Be: It, There, and the Past Tense of Be

15 Practice

Answer questions about your hometown.

1. What's the weather like in the winter?

   _____.

2. Is it hot in the summer?

   _____.

3. Are there mountains near your hometown?

   _____.

4. How many parks are there in your hometown?

   _____.

5. How many rivers are there?

   _____.

6. Is there a subway?

   _____.

2f The Conjunctions *And, But,* and *Or*

Student Book p. 48

16 Practice

Complete the sentences with *and, but,* or *or*.

1. Are those apples _____ oranges?

2. Apples are red _____ white.

3. In the winter, my town is sunny _____ cold.

4. Do you want soup, _____ do you want a salad?

5. This class is crowded _____ good.

6. Do you think the food tastes sweet _____ salty?

7. The book is good, _____ it is long.

8. From the station, there are trains _____ no buses.

9. I have class from 8:00 A.M. to 5:00 P.M. I have class in the

   morning _____ the afternoon.

10. My mother has cats _____ dogs.

11. Do you like yellow _____ blue?

12. The doctor is smart, _____ she is friendly.

17 Practice

Match the ideas. Then write sentences with *and, but,* or *or*. Use commas correctly.

A.

___b___ **1.** She speaks Korean   **a.** I'm not tired.

_____ **2.** It's 2:00 A.M.   **b.** English.

_____ **3.** My best friend is smart   **c.** Monday?

_____ **4.** It's summer   **d.** it's cold.

_____ **5.** Are lemons sweet   **e.** small.

_____ **6.** Do you want to see the movie on Saturday   **f.** are they sour?

_____ **7.** The kitchen is clean   **g.** funny.

_____ **8.** I study hard   **h.** I make good grades.

B.

1. _She speaks Korean and English_ _____.

2. _____.

3. _____.

4. _____.

5. _____.

6. _____.

7. _____.

8. _____.

18 **Practice**

Complete the sentences with your ideas.

1. *I am not rich, but I'm hardworking* _____ .

2. I _____ and _____ .

3. I _____ but _____ .

4. I _____ and _____ .

5. My best friend _____ but _____ .

6. My best friend _____ and _____ .

2g The Past Tense of *Be*: Affirmative and Negative Statements

Student Book p. 51

19 **Practice**

Complete the sentences with *is, was, are,* or *were*.

1. I _____ single in 2000.

2. Today, I _____ married.

3. In 1999, my husband _____ 190 pounds.

4. Today, he _____ 165 pounds.

5. We _____ in Canada in 1998.

6. My husband _____ an engineer in Toronto.

7. Today, we _____ in Japan.

8. I _____ an English teacher now.

20 **Practice**

Complete the sentences with *wasn't* or *weren't*.

1. Ron was at a baseball game yesterday. He ___*wasn't*___ in the office.

2. He _____ by himself. He was with his friends.

3. They were also at the game. They _____ at the office either.

4. They _____ busy with work. They were relaxed.

5. It was a day off for them. It _____ a regular workday.

6. They _____ in suits. They were in shorts and T-shirts.

Practice

Complete the sentences with *was* or *were*.

Martin Luther King, Jr.
American
Civil rights worker
Died 39
Married

Mahatma Gandhi
Indian
Civil rights worker
Died 77
Married

Martin Luther King, Jr. and Mahatma Gandhi _____*were*_____ both civil rights

workers. Martin Luther King, Jr. _____ American and Mahatma Gandhi

          1

_____ was Indian. They _____ both married. Dr. King

    3   4

_____ 39 when he died, and Gandhi _____ 77 when he died.

    5   6

People _____ sad. They _____ good men.

         7   8

2h The Past Tense of *Be:* Questions

Student Book p. 54

22 Practice

Ask and answer questions about a movie at a new theater using the prompts.

1. the movie/good _____*Was the movie good*_____ ?

   Yes, _____*it was*_____ .

2. the theater/clean _____ ?

   No, _____ .

3. it/busy _____ ?

   Yes, _____ .

4. theater/big _____ ?

   No, _____ .

5. food/expensive _____ ?

   Yes, _____ .

6. workers/polite _____ ?

   Yes, _____ .

Be: It, There, and the Past Tense of *Be*

Practice

Ask and answer the questions using the prompts.

1. hot/yesterday

   Was it hot yesterday _____?

   No, it wasn't _____ (OR) _Yes, it was_ _____.

2. your room/clean/last week

   _____?

   _____.

3. the homework/difficult/yesterday

   _____?

   _____.

4. your friends/in school/today

   _____?

   _____.

5. your last birthday/fun

   _____?

   _____.

6. your computer/expensive

   _____?

   _____.

7. the bands/loud/last night

   _____?

   _____.

24 Practice

Match the questions with the answers.

Questions		Answers
_e_ **1.** How old were you in 1990?		**a.** In Argentina.
_____ **2.** What was your puppy's name?		**b.** No, it wasn't. It was Louise.
_____ **3.** Was your favorite color yellow?		**c.** It was in September.
_____ **4.** Where were you born?		**d.** His name was Rover.
_____ **5.** Was your best friend's name Mary?		**e.** I was nine years old.
_____ **6.** When was your first day of class?		**f.** Yes, it was.

25 Practice

Write questions and answers using the prompts.

1. when/you/born

When were you born ?

I was born on March 20, 1983 .

2. where/you/born

_____ ?

_____ .

3. when/your last birthday

_____ ?

_____ .

4. how old/you/on your last birthday

_____ ?

_____ .

5. where/you/two hours ago

_____ ?

_____ .

6. where/your best friend/three days ago

_____ ?

_____ .

Be: It, There, and the Past Tense of Be

SELF-TEST

A **Choose the best answer, A, B, C, or D, to complete the sentence. Mark your answer by darkening the oval with the same letter.**

1. What time is _____?

   A. it   Ⓐ Ⓑ Ⓒ Ⓓ
   B. day
   C. they
   D. date

2. I have class _____ the morning.

   A. at   Ⓐ Ⓑ Ⓒ Ⓓ
   B. on
   C. to
   D. in

3. How many dogs _____ in the park today?

   A. is there   Ⓐ Ⓑ Ⓒ Ⓓ
   B. there are
   C. there is
   D. are there

4. There _____ two cups on the table.

   A. is   Ⓐ Ⓑ Ⓒ Ⓓ
   B. was
   C. are
   D. wasn't

5. _____ there a park near here?

   A. Is   Ⓐ Ⓑ Ⓒ Ⓓ
   B. Are
   C. Aren't
   D. Were

6. She speaks Italian, French, _____ Spanish.

   A. or   Ⓐ Ⓑ Ⓒ Ⓓ
   B. and
   C. from
   D. but

7. Janet _____ a secretary 30 years ago.

   A. are   Ⓐ Ⓑ Ⓒ Ⓓ
   B. was
   C. is
   D. were

8. Max and Sherry _____ happy today.

   A. are   Ⓐ Ⓑ Ⓒ Ⓓ
   B. was
   C. is
   D. were

9. Where _____ you born?

   A. are   Ⓐ Ⓑ Ⓒ Ⓓ
   B. was
   C. is
   D. were

10. Alan was at home yesterday. He _____ at his office.

    A. aren't   Ⓐ Ⓑ Ⓒ Ⓓ
    B. wasn't
    C. isn't
    D. weren't

B **Find the underlined word or phrase, A, B, C, or D, that is incorrect. Mark your answer by darkening the oval with the same letter.**

1. What are the temperature in Miami today?
     A   B   C   D

   Ⓐ Ⓑ Ⓒ Ⓓ

2. What time are it now?
     A   B   C D

   Ⓐ Ⓑ Ⓒ Ⓓ

3. The party is at 2:00 on the afternoon.
         A   B C   D

   Ⓐ Ⓑ Ⓒ Ⓓ

4. I have class from 9:00 in 3:30
     A   B   C

   in the afternoon.
     D

   Ⓐ Ⓑ Ⓒ Ⓓ

5. There is books on the table.
     A B C   D

   Ⓐ Ⓑ Ⓒ Ⓓ

6. Are there any shop in town?
     A   B   C   D

   Ⓐ Ⓑ Ⓒ Ⓓ

7. How many rooms are they in the hotel?
     A   B C   D

   Ⓐ Ⓑ Ⓒ Ⓓ

8. My teacher is nice, or she gives us a lot
     A   B   C   D
   of homework.

   Ⓐ Ⓑ Ⓒ Ⓓ

9. Peg and Bob was engineers 50 years ago.
        A   B   C   D

   Ⓐ Ⓑ Ⓒ Ⓓ

10. Where were you in your last birthday?
       A   B   C D

    Ⓐ Ⓑ Ⓒ Ⓓ

UNIT 3
THE SIMPLE PRESENT TENSE

3a The Simple Present Tense
Student Book p. 62

☐ Practice

Read the sentences about Jack and underline the correct form of the verbs in parentheses.

1. Jack (get / <u>gets</u>) up at 6:30 A.M. every day.

2. Then, he (take / takes) a shower and (comb / combs) his hair.

3. Jack (live / lives) with his brother, Danny.

4. Jack and Danny (eat / eats) breakfast and (drink / drinks) tea.

5. They (talk / talks) for a few minutes, and then they (leave / leaves) the house at different times.

6. Jack (get / gets) on his bus at 8:00.

7. Jack (work / works) for a TV station.

8. He really (like / likes) his job.

9. Danny (walk / walks) to work at 8:15.

10. He (teach / teaches) music at a school near their house.

11. Jack and Danny (get / gets) home about the same time every day.

12. At night, Danny (call / calls) his friends.

13. They (say / says) good night about 11:00.

14. Jack (dream / dreams) about his next vacation.

2 Practice

Write what you and your best friend do every day.

Me	My Best Friend
I _____eat breakfast at 7:30._____	My best friend _watches TV_ at 9:00 P.M.
I _____ at 10:30 A.M.	My best friend _____ at 8:30 P.M.
I _____ at 4:00 P.M.	She/He _____ _____ .
I _____ _____ .	She/He _____ _____ .
I _____ _____ .	She/He _____ _____ .

3b Adverbs of Frequency

Student Book p. 64

3 Practice

Add the adverbs of frequency to the sentences.

1. My husband gets up at 5:30 A.M.

   (always) _My husband always gets up at 5:30 A.M._

2. We eat breakfast together.

   (rarely) _____ .

3. I drink coffee.

(usually) _____.

4. My husband drinks coffee.

(never) _____.

5. I read the newspaper.

(often) _____.

6. My husband drives to work.

(sometimes) _____.

7. My husband takes a lunch with him.

(always) _____.

8. I buy my lunch.

(often) _____.

9. I see my husband in the day.

(rarely) _____.

10. We stay home Saturday night.

(never) _____.

4 | Practice

Circle an adverb to complete each sentence about you and your friends.

1. I (always / usually / often / sometimes / rarely / never) sleep in the day.

2. I (always / usually / often / sometimes / rarely / never) eat breakfast.

3. I (always / usually / often / sometimes / rarely / never) do my homework.

4. I (always / usually / often / sometimes / rarely / never) watch TV.

5. My friends (always / usually / often / sometimes / rarely / never) go dancing.

6. My friends (always / usually / often / sometimes / rarely / never) drive.

7. I (always / usually / often / sometimes / rarely / never) go to bed late.

8. I (always / usually / often / sometimes / rarely / never) talk on the phone.

9. I (always / usually / often / sometimes / rarely / never) take the bus.

10. My best friend (always / usually / often / sometimes / rarely / never) exercises.

5 Practice

Complete the sentences about you, your family, and your friends.

1. I always _____ *take a shower in the morning* _____.

2. I never _____.

3. My best friend usually _____.

4. My best friend always _____.

5. He/She rarely _____.

6. My mom and dad often _____.

7. My sister(s)/brother(s) sometimes _____.

8. My sister(s)/brother(s) usually _____.

9. My teacher often _____.

10. He/She never _____.

3c Adverbs of Frequency with *Be*

Student Book p. 66

6 Practice

Write *C* next to the sentence if the adverb is in the correct place. Write *I* if the adverb is in the incorrect place.

1. __*I*__ I always am late.

2. __*C*__ We usually drive.

3. _____ They never go to bed early.

4. _____ Tony is often lazy.

5. _____ My father calls usually me on Sunday.

6. _____ We are rarely tired.

7. _____ My wife and I sometimes watch TV at night.

8. _____ Jack works sometimes in his garden.

9. _____ Sylvia rarely is at home.

10. _____ It often rains in the winter.

7 Practice

Add the adverbs of frequency to the following sentences about Sharon.

1. Sharon works out at the gym. (always)

   Sharon always works out at the gym .

2. Sharon calls her mother. (always)

   _____ .

3. Sharon is late. (never)

   _____ .

4. Sharon drinks tea. (often)

   _____ .

5. She feels tired. (rarely)

   _____ .

6. She eats pizza. (sometimes)

   _____ .

7. Sharon is home in the afternoon. (usually)

   _____ .

8. She is tired in the evening. (sometimes)

   _____ .

9. Sharon has fun with her family. (often)

   _____ .

10. Sharon and her brother are happy. (usually)

   _____ .

3d Spelling and Pronunciation of Final –s and –es
Student Book p. 68

8 Practice

Circle the correct form of the verbs in parentheses.

1. Jennifer (gets / getes) up every day at 6:00.

2. Jennifer (washs / washes) her hair every day.

3. She (drinks / drinkes) coffee with her breakfast.

4. She (brushs / brushes) her teeth.

5. She (fixs / fixes) lunch and (kisss / kisses) her children goodbye.

6. She (begins / begines) work at 7:00.

7. Jennifer (staies / stays) at work until 5:00.

8. She (walks / walkes) home.

9. Jennifer (makes / makees) dinner for her family.

10. She (watchs / watches) TV.

11. She (puts / putes) her children to bed.

12. Jennifer (studys / studies) a little English at night.

13. Jennifer (speaks / speakes) three languages.

14. She (sleeps / sleepes) seven hours every night.

9 Practice

Complete the sentences with the correct form of the verbs in parentheses. Then circle the correct pronunciation for each.

My best friend, Ysabel, (come) ____*comes*____ (s / z / iz) from Venezuela and
                                        1

(speak) _____ (s / z / iz) Spanish and English. She (live) _____
                  2   3

(s / z / iz) in the United States now, but she (miss) _____ (s / z / iz) her
                                                                4

friends in Caracas very much. Ysabel (dance) _____ (s / z / iz) very well. She
                                                          5

(enjoy) _____ (s / z / iz) music. She (play) _____ (s / z / iz) guitar
              6   7

every day. She always (listen) _____ (s / z / iz) to the radio. Ysabel rarely
                                        8

(watch) _____ (s / z / iz) TV.
                9

10 Practice

Complete the sentences about Peter with the words in parentheses. Some sentences use the verb *be*.

1. Peter (always, study) ____*always studies*____ hard.

2. Peter (often, play) _____ tennis.

3. He (sometimes, cook) _____ dinner

   for his friends.

4. Peter (usually, be) _____ happy.

5. He (often, laugh) _____ .

6. He (rarely, worry) _____ about things.

7. Peter (never, watch) _____ TV.

8. He (be) _____ nice to animals and children.

9. He (love) _____ his brothers and sisters.

10. Peter (always, brush) _____ his teeth after dinner.

3e Irregular Verbs: *Have*, *Do*, and *Go*
Student Book p. 71

11 Practice
Complete the sentences about Joan and Phil with the words in parentheses.

1. Phil and Joan (have) _____ *have* _____ a nice life.

2. Phil (go) _____ to work every morning at 7:30.

3. Phil (do) _____ aerobics at the gym in the evening.

4. Joan (have) _____ a good job in a hospital.

5. Because they both work, they both (clean) _____ the house.

6. Joan (do) _____ the gardening, and Phil

(do) _____ the dishes.

7. Joan (go) _____ to Florida every winter to visit her father.

3f *Have* and *Has*
Student Book p. 73

12 Practice
Complete the sentences with *have* or *has*.

Cindy _____ *has* _____ a brother, John. They both _____ good jobs.
₁ ₂

Cindy _____ a new house. John _____ an apartment. The apartment
₃ ₄

_____ one bedroom. It also _____ a large kitchen. Cindy and John
₅ ₆

sometimes _____ dinner together.
₇

13 Practice

Complete with _have/has_ or _is/are_.

1. Mark ___is___ a student.
2. He _____ a brother, Max.
3. Mark and Max _____ very nice.
4. They _____ different.
5. They _____ a good time together.

6. Max _____ a musician.
7. Max _____ a guitar.
8. Today, Max _____ a headache.
9. Mark and Max _____ brown hair.
10. They _____ happy.

14 Practice

Describe yourself and your best friend.

Me	My Best Friend
I have brown hair.	_She/He has blue eyes._
I have a sister.	

3g The Simple Present Tense: Negative
Student Book p. 75

15 Practice

Complete the negative sentences using the words in parentheses.

1. I have a sister, but I (not, have) _____don't have_____ any brothers.

2. My sister likes sandwiches, but she (not, eat) _____ pizza.

3. She likes water, but she (not, drink) _____ tea.

4. We study English together, but we (not, speak) _____ it very well.

5. Our parents like music, but they (not, watch) _____ TV very much.

6. My dad has a computer, but he (not, use) _____ it.

7. My mom uses the computer, but she (not, go) _____ on the Internet.

8. I wash clothes, but I (not, wash) _____ the dishes.

16 Practice

Write true sentences using the following prompts. Make the sentences negative where necessary.

1. babies/drive

    Babies don't drive   .

2. chickens/lay/eggs

    Chickens lay eggs   .

3. kangaroos/live/in Australia

    _____ .

4. flowers/talk

    _____ .

5. it/snow/Cuba

    _____ .

6. a house/fly

    _____ .

7. a penguin/speak English

    _____ .

8. whales/live/in trees

    _____ .

9. the sun/come up/in the morning

    _____ .

10. a panda/play/the guitar

    _____ .

17 Practice

Complete the sentences with the negative form of the verbs from the list.

ask	feel	have	like	talk
eat	go	know	sleep	understand

Bruno is from Italy. He _doesn't feel_ very well. He _____

the food here, so he _____ very much. He's alone a lot because he

_____ any friends. He _____ to the other

students in his class. He _____ out at night. He just stays in his

room. Bruno _____ very well. He's always tired. His roommates

_____ what to do. They _____ Bruno to do things

with them because he always says no. They _____ why he is so sad.

18 Practice

Write three things you do and three things you don't do on Saturday. Use phrases from the list or your own.

do homework	go to parties	play football	work
get up early	go to school	sleep late	wash clothes

1. _I don't go to school. I see my friends_____.

2. _____.

3. _____.

4. _____.

5. _____.

6. _____.

3h The Simple Present Tense: Yes/No Questions

Student Book p. 78

19 Practice

Answer the questions using short answers.

1. Do you like cars? _Yes, I do_____.

2. Are you tired? _No, I'm not_____.

3. Do you watch football? _____.

4. Do you have a husband or a wife? _____.

5. Does your teacher give you a lot of homework? _____.

6. Is your best friend happy? _____.

7. Do you swim? _____.

8. Do you read a newspaper every day? _____.

9. Do you have a computer? _____.

10. Are you good at English? _____.

20 Practice

Jeff and Andrea don't know each other very well. Write their questions and answers using words from the chart or your own.

Jeff	Andrea
plays guitar	likes reading newspapers
has animals	is from Italy
only speaks English	works at home
lives in an apartment	has her own house
watches TV	enjoys movies
doesn't read newspapers	likes music and animals

Jeff: _Do you speak any other languages_____?

Andrea: _Yes, I do. I speak Italian_____.

Andrea: _Do you speak any other languages_____?

Jeff: _No, I don't_____.

Jeff: _____?

Andrea: _____.

Andrea: _____?

Jeff: _____.

Jeff: _____?

Andrea: _____.

Andrea: _____?

Jeff: _____.

Jeff: _____?

Andrea: _____.

Andrea: _____?

Jeff: _____.

Jeff: _____?

Andrea: _____.

Andrea: _____?

Jeff: _____.

The Simple Present Tense

21 Practice

Read about Anita and Pablo. Then write ten questions and short answers with _am_, _is_, _do_, or _does_.

This is Anita and Pablo. They are friends, and they live in Boston. Pablo is an English teacher, and Anita is a lawyer. Anita lives with a roommate, and Pablo lives with his mother. Pablo teaches English in a school. He loves his job. Anita works a lot. For fun, Anita likes to run. Pablo likes to go to movies. Pablo laughs a lot. He is fun. I like Anita and Pablo very much.

1. _Are Anita and Pablo friends? Yes, they are_____.
2. _Do they live in San Francisco? No, they don't_____.
3. _____.
4. _____.
5. _____.
6. _____.
7. _____.
8. _____.
9. _____.
10. _____.

3i The Simple Present Tense: Wh- Questions
Student Book p. 80

22 Practice

Write _C_ if the statement is correct. Write _I_ if the statement is incorrect.

1. __C__ Where do you live?

2. __I__ What does they want?

3. _____ How many bedrooms do it have?

4. _____ Where does she come from?

5. _____ When do you come home?

6. _____ What do it eat?

7. _____ Why do you drive to work?

8. _____ When does she get up?

9. _____ How many friends does you have?

23 Practice

Read about Mary Barnes. Then write questions and answers using the prompts.

Mary Barnes lives in Canada. Mary is a nurse. She works in a hospital. She likes Canada because there aren't a lot of people there. The sun shines all day in the summer, but in the winter it is very cold. She is married to Michael. Michael works at a gas station. They walk and play music for fun. Mary and Michael have three children. Their son lives near them. One of their daughters is an accountant, and their other daughter stays home with her baby boy.

1. where/Mary/live

Where does Mary live ?

She lives in Canada .

2. what/she/do

_____ ?

_____ .

3. where/she/work

_____ ?

_____ .

4. why/she/like Canada

_____ ?

_____ .

5. what/sun/do/summer

_____?

_____.

6. what/is/weather/like in winter

_____?

_____.

7. where/Michael/work

_____?

_____.

8. what/they/do/for fun

_____?

_____.

9. how many/children/they/have

_____?

_____.

10. where/son/live

_____?

_____.

11. what/one daughter/do

_____?

_____.

12. who/stay home/with baby

_____?

_____.

24 Practice

This is Walter. He's an accountant. Match the questions with the answers.

1. _____ What does he do?
2. _____ Where does he live?
3. _____ How many children does he have?
4. _____ When does he work?
5. _____ When does he leave in the morning?
6. _____ Who does he live with?
7. _____ Why does he live in Florida?
8. _____ What does he do at night?

a. Works on his car.
b. He doesn't like cold weather.
c. His wife and children.
d. In Miami.
e. He's an accountant.
f. Two.
g. In the daytime.
h. At 7:30.

25 Practice

Complete the questions with *is*, *are*, *do*, or *does*.

1. How _____*do*_____ bees make food?

   They get nectar from flowers.

2. What _____ nectar?

   It's a combination of water and sugars.

3. How many kinds of bees _____ there in their home? There are three kinds: workers, drones, and the queen.

4. What _____ the queen do?

   She makes eggs.

5. _____ the queen big?

   Yes, she's the biggest bee in the group.

6. How _____ bees talk to each other?

   They dance and the other bees understand what they are saying.

26 Practice

Write questions for these answers about capybaras.

1. _What's that animal_ _____?

    It's a capybara.

2. _____?

    It lives in Central and South America.

3. _____?

    They eat plants.

4. _____?

    Yes, they live in groups of about 10–20.

5. _____?

    A capybara lives for seven to ten years.

6. _____?

    They have four to five babies.

7. _____?

    Yes, they live on land and in water.

8. _____?

    Yes, they swim.

SELF-TEST

A Choose the best answer, A, B, C, or D, to complete the sentence. Mark your answer by darkening the oval with the same letter.

1. Jackson _____ early.

   A. get up   Ⓐ Ⓑ Ⓒ Ⓓ
   B. gets up never
   C. never gets up
   D. never

2. How many teeth _____ a person have?

   A. do   Ⓐ Ⓑ Ⓒ Ⓓ
   B. does
   C. are
   D. is

3. Pusan _____ a city in Korea.

   A. do   Ⓐ Ⓑ Ⓒ Ⓓ
   B. does
   C. are
   D. is

4. Penguins _____ fly.

   A. don't   Ⓐ Ⓑ Ⓒ Ⓓ
   B. doesn't
   C. isn't
   D. aren't

5. It _____ here in the winter.

   A. rain often   Ⓐ Ⓑ Ⓒ Ⓓ
   B. often rain
   C. often rains
   D. often

6. Where _____ coffee come from?

   A. do   Ⓐ Ⓑ Ⓒ Ⓓ
   B. does
   C. are
   D. is

7. A person _____ one head.

   A. do   Ⓐ Ⓑ Ⓒ Ⓓ
   B. does
   C. have
   D. has

8. Lisa _____ in the morning.

   A. always exercises   Ⓐ Ⓑ Ⓒ Ⓓ
   B. always is
   C. exercises always
   D. always has

9. My teacher _____ tired.

   A. always is   Ⓐ Ⓑ Ⓒ Ⓓ
   B. always does
   C. is always
   D. always do

10. The sun _____ in the night.

    A. comes up never   Ⓐ Ⓑ Ⓒ Ⓓ
    B. never comes up
    C. don't come up
    D. doesn't comes up

B Find the underlined word or phrase, A, B, C, or D, that is incorrect. Mark your answer by darkening the oval with the same letter.

1. <u>Does</u> <u>there</u> <u>24 hours</u> <u>in a</u> day?
      A   B   C   D

   Ⓐ Ⓑ Ⓒ Ⓓ

2. <u>Pandas</u> <u>eat always</u> <u>bamboo</u> and <u>live</u>
      A   B   C   D
   in China.

   Ⓐ Ⓑ Ⓒ Ⓓ

3. Stan <u>usually</u> <u>get up</u> <u>at 7:00</u>
            A   B   C
   <u>during the week</u>.
         D

   Ⓐ Ⓑ Ⓒ Ⓓ

4. <u>How many</u> <u>languages</u> <u>do</u> she <u>speak</u>?
       A   B   C   D

   Ⓐ Ⓑ Ⓒ Ⓓ

5. <u>Does</u> kangaroos <u>live</u> in North America, or
     A   B
   <u>do they</u> <u>live</u> in Australia?
     C   D

   Ⓐ Ⓑ Ⓒ Ⓓ

6. Joe <u>like</u> coffee, <u>but</u> <u>he</u> <u>doesn't</u> like tea.
       A   B C   D

   Ⓐ Ⓑ Ⓒ Ⓓ

7. San Francisco <u>has</u> <u>cold</u> in the <u>summer</u>, but
              A   B   C
   <u>it's</u> nice in the spring.
    D

   Ⓐ Ⓑ Ⓒ Ⓓ

8. I <u>doesn't</u> watch TV, but <u>I</u> <u>usually</u> <u>listen</u>
      A   B   C   D
   to music.

   Ⓐ Ⓑ Ⓒ Ⓓ

9. <u>How many</u> books <u>do</u> <u>you</u> <u>has</u>?
      A   B C D

   Ⓐ Ⓑ Ⓒ Ⓓ

10. <u>How many</u> times a day <u>are</u> you <u>usually</u>
       A   B   C
    <u>talk</u> on the telephone?
     D

    Ⓐ Ⓑ Ⓒ Ⓓ

UNIT 4
THE PRESENT PROGRESSIVE TENSE

4a The Present Progressive Tense: Affirmative Statements
Student Book p. 92

1 **Practice**

Complete the sentences with the present progressive tense of the verbs in parentheses.

1. The children (play) _are playing._

2. Jason (walk) _____ in the park.

3. Dave (lock) _____ his car.

4. Sylvia (wash) _____ the windows in her house.

5. Kyle (wait) _____ for the bus.

6. Birds (fly) _____ in the sky.

7. Matt (fix) _____ his bicycle.

8. Two girls (talk) _____.

9. A baby (cry) _____.

10. Two boys (eat) _____ sandwiches.

11. A man and a woman (go) _____ to the movie theater.

12. A girl (climb) _____ a tree.

13. A man (sleep) _____ under the tree.

14. The man (wear) _____ a hat.

15. A woman (sit) _____ and (work) _____

on her computer.

2 Practice

Look at the photos. Write what the people are doing.

1. _The people are singing_____.

_____.

2. _____.

_____.

3. _____.

_____.

3 | Practice

Describe what your family is doing and wearing now.

1. *I'm doing my homework* _____.

2. I _____.

3. I _____.

4. My mother _____.

5. My mother _____.

6. My father _____.

7. My father _____.

8. My brother/sister _____.

9. My brother/sister _____.

4b The Spelling of Verbs Ending in -*ing*
Student Book p. 97

4 | Practice

Write the -*ing* form of each verb.

1. give _____
2. swim _____
3. worry _____
4. carry _____
5. grow _____
6. dance _____
7. come _____
8. kiss _____
9. eat _____
10. fix _____

11. write _____
12. sleep _____
13. read _____
14. type _____
15. say _____
16. drive _____
17. study _____
18. wear _____
19. rain _____
20. stop _____

5 Practice

Complete the sentences with the present progressive of the verbs in parentheses.

1. Dad (make) _____ dinner.

2. He (plan) _____ my mother's birthday party for tomorrow.

3. My mother (drive) _____ to the store now.

4. I (relax) _____ in my room.

5. My sister (put) _____ on a hat.

6. My brother (read) _____ a book and

   (write) _____ a letter.

7. He (type) _____ it.

8. He (hurry) _____. He has a soccer game tonight.

9. I (sit) _____ on my bed and

   (look) _____ out the window.

10. I (think) _____ about my future.

6 Practice

Complete the sentences with the present progressive of the verbs from the list. Use the correct spelling.

check	look	read	snow	take	write
eat	look at	sit	stand	think	yawn

Dear Krystal,

   I ____'m sitting____ in my English class and I _____ of you.
          1   2
We _____ a test. The teacher _____ in front of the
          3   4
class, and she _____ a book.
                      5
   My classmates are funny. Steve _____ out the window. It
                                              6
_____. Melinda _____ because she is tired, and Diane
          7   8
is _____ an apple. Bill and Ann _____ letters, too.
          9   10
Chelsea _____ messages on her phone.
              11
   The teacher _____ me now.
                      12
Write soon,

Laurie

7 | Practice

Complete the sentences with the present progressive of the verbs in parentheses.

It's a great day! The sun (shine) _____is shining_____. The flowers

(grow) _____. In the park, boys (run) _____ and

some girls (play) _____ music and (sing) _____.

Children (ride) _____ their bicycles.

8 | Practice

Write eight sentences about what is happening in your house right now. You may use verbs from the list or your own.

dance	listen to music	read a book	watch TV
do homework	play video games	talk to friends	wear a coat

1. _My father is working right now_____.
2. _____.
3. _____.
4. _____.
5. _____.
6. _____.
7. _____.
8. _____.

9 | Practice

Write C next to the word if the -ing is correct. Write I if the -ing is incorrect.

1. __I__ swiming   5. _____ hurrying

2. __C__ saying   6. _____ smiling

3. _____ planning   7. _____ writeing

4. _____ siting   8. _____ giving

The Present Progressive Tense: Negative Statements

Student Book p. 100

10 Practice

Read the statements. Then write negative statements using the prompts.

1. My sister is sleeping.

   she/not/work _She isn't working._____ (OR) _She's not working_____.

2. It's sunny now.

   it/not/rain _____.

3. I'm watching TV.

   I/not/do homework _____.

4. I'm studying English.

   I/not/study Italian _____.

5. My mom is reading.

   she/not/make lunch _____.

6. Danny is carrying a briefcase.

   he/not/carry a handbag _____.

7. Jerry is fixing his motorcycle.

   he/not/ride it _____.

8. We're opening the door.

   we/not/close it _____.

11 Practice

Look at the photos. Read the statements. Write correct negative statements.

1. A woman is swimming. _A woman isn't swimming_____.

   _A man is carrying his son_____.

2. The man is wearing a hat.

   _____.

   _____.

3. The man is crying.

   _____.

   _____.

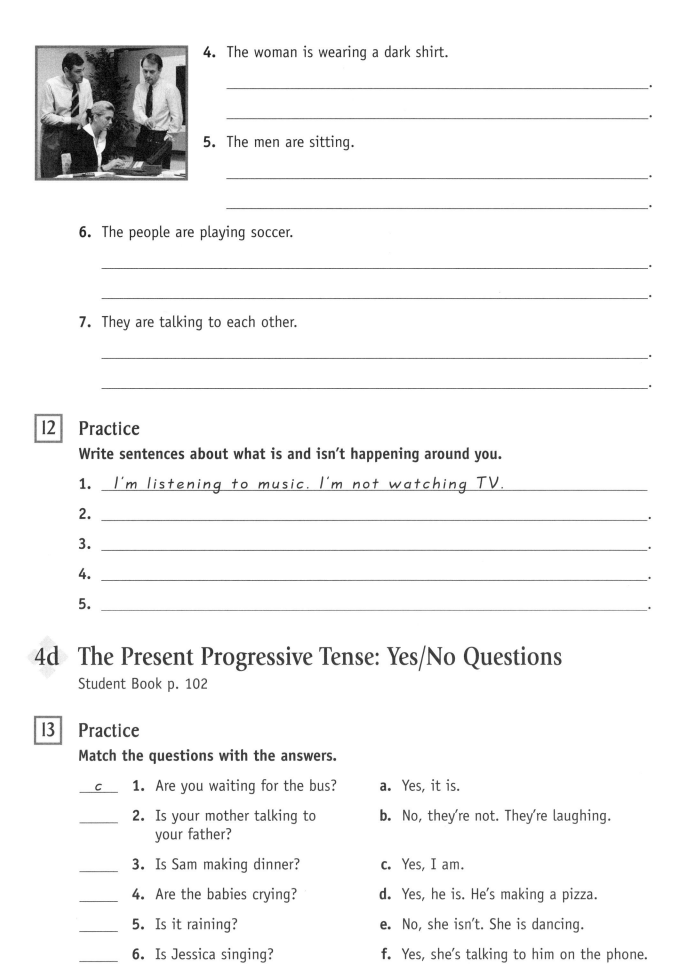

4. The woman is wearing a dark shirt.

_____ .

_____ .

5. The men are sitting.

_____ .

_____ .

6. The people are playing soccer.

_____ .

_____ .

7. They are talking to each other.

_____ .

_____ .

|12| **Practice**

Write sentences about what is and isn't happening around you.

1. _I'm listening to music. I'm not watching TV._ _____

2. _____ .

3. _____ .

4. _____ .

5. _____ .

4d The Present Progressive Tense: Yes/No Questions

Student Book p. 102

|13| **Practice**

Match the questions with the answers.

_c_ **1.** Are you waiting for the bus?   **a.** Yes, it is.

____ **2.** Is your mother talking to your father?   **b.** No, they're not. They're laughing.

____ **3.** Is Sam making dinner?   **c.** Yes, I am.

____ **4.** Are the babies crying?   **d.** Yes, he is. He's making a pizza.

____ **5.** Is it raining?   **e.** No, she isn't. She is dancing.

____ **6.** Is Jessica singing?   **f.** Yes, she's talking to him on the phone.

Read the answers and write questions using the present progressive tense. You may use phrases from the list to help you.

cry	go to work	make dinner	watch TV
drive to school	have a big dinner	pick up	
go to bed	have a good time	visit New York City	

1. _Is Jack crying_ _____?

   No, he isn't. He's smiling.

2. _Are they having a big dinner_ _____?

   Yes, they are. They're hungry.

3. _____?

   No, she isn't. She's driving to work.

4. _____?

   Yes, we are. We're on vacation!

5. _____?

   No, I'm not. I'm not tired.

6. _____?

   Yes, you are. You have the car!

7. _____?

   No, they're not. They don't like big cities.

8. _____?

   No, she isn't. She's staying home today.

9. _____?

   Yes, he is. He likes to cook.

10. _____?

    No, they're not. They're playing video games.

4e The Present Progressive Tense: Wh- Questions

Student Book p. 105

15 **Practice**

Write a question for each sentence. Use the wh- question words in parentheses.

1. She's driving a bus. (what)

   What is she driving ?

2. I'm making popcorn. (what)

   _____ ?

3. Ken is writing a book. (who)

   _____ ?

4. Mary Ann is talking to the children. (who)

   _____ ?

5. I'm wearing a hat. (what)

   _____ ?

6. Sam is watching TV. (what)

   _____ ?

7. The children are going to the library. (where)

   _____ ?

8. Ryan and Sarah are going to the movie theater. (where)

   _____ ?

9. Wendy isn't feeling well. (how)

   _____ ?

10. Scott is swimming. (what)

    _____ ?

Practice

Look at the photos and write questions for the sentences. The underlined words are the answers.

1. The family is <u>eating lunch</u>.

   What is the family doing ?

2. They are sitting <u>in the kitchen</u>.

   _____

   _____?

3. Their father is <u>pouring milk</u>.

   _____?

4. The children are <u>looking at their bowls</u>.

   _____?

5. The mother is <u>wearing a t-shirt</u>.

   _____?

6. They're going <u>home</u>.

   _____

   _____?

7. They're going <u>by train</u>.

   _____

   _____?

8. They're feeling <u>tired</u>.

   _____?

9. The woman is <u>sleeping</u>.

   _____?

10. <u>The man</u> is looking out the window.

    _____?

4f Verbs Not Used in the Present Progressive Tense

Student Book p. 108

17 **Practice**

Complete the sentences with the simple present or present progressive of the verbs in parentheses.

Kurt: What (do) _____*are*_____ you _____*doing*_____?
          (1)

Liz: I (make) _____ a cake.
          2

Kurt: It (smell) _____ good!
          3

Liz: Where (go) _____ you _____?
          4   (4)

Kurt.   The store.

Liz: I (need) _____ eggs.
          5

Kurt: Okay.

Melissa: What (do) _____ you _____ right now?
          6   (6)

Ricky: I (study) _____ and (listen) _____ to music.
          7   8

          What (do) _____ you _____?
          9   (9)

Melissa: I (have) _____ a new DVD, and I
          10

          (watch) _____ it. (want) _____ you
          11   12

          _____ to come to my house?
          (12)

Ricky: Sure!

Eric: I (like) _____ our English class.
          13

Gwen: Really? I (not, understand) _____ the homework.
          14

Eric: I (do) _____ it right now. It's not difficult.
          15

Practice

Look at the photo and complete the sentences with verbs from the list. You may use a verb more than one time. Use the simple present or present progressive.

be
have
look at
wear

Today _____ Flora's birthday. Her family
                    1

_____ a party. They _____ a party every year.
        2   3

Her husband _____ a blue shirt and Flora _____
                        4   5

a pink shirt. Flora _____ blond hair. The family
                              6

_____ at the cake. They _____ a good time.
          7   8

19 Practice

Look at the following pairs. Only one sentence is possible. Circle the letter of the correct sentence.

1. **a.** Sandy is not understanding the question.
   b. Sandy doesn't understand the question.

2. **a.** This popcorn is tasting good.
   b. This popcorn tastes good.

3. **a.** I'm remembering you.
   b. I remember you.

4. **a.** Look! Those men are singing.
   b. Look! Those men sing.

5. **a.** It's raining now.
   b. It's rains now.

6. **a.** I'm hating homework.
   b. I hate homework.

[20] **Practice**

Complete the sentences with the words in parentheses. Use contractions when possible.

1. A: (know) _____*Do*_____ you _____*know*_____ Mr. Lee?

   B: Sure. I (remember) _____ him. He

   (teach) _____ history. My brother (take) _____

   his class now.

2. A: What (do) _____ Patty _____?

   B: She (work) _____ with a student now.

   A: Why?

   B: He (not, understand) _____ the homework.

3. A: Why (cry) _____ you _____?

   B: I (watch) _____ a sad movie.

   A: I (not, like) _____ sad movies.

4. A: My husband (make) _____ dinner.

   B: (usually, make) _____ he _____ dinner?

   A: No, I (usually, make) _____ it, but I

   (have) _____ a meeting. I (leave) _____ now.

5. A: Hi, what (do) _____ you _____?

   B: I (study) _____. What (do) _____

   you _____?

   A: Not much.

6. A: (like) _____ you _____ pizza?

   B: Yes, I (do) _____, but I (prefer) _____ salad.

7. A: Hey, (hear) _____ you _____ that?

   B: Yes, it (rain) _____.

8. A: Why (laugh) _____ your brother _____?

   B: He (think) _____ he is funny.

9. A: What (usually, do) _____ you _____

after school?

B: I (run) _____. You?

A: I (usually, go) _____ to the store, but today I

(go) _____ to the doctor's.

10. A: Why (wait) _____ you _____ for the bus?

B: I (not, have) _____ a car. I

(usually, take) _____ the bus.

11. Susan (talk) _____ on the phone because she

(not, like) _____ her homework exercise. She

(sit) _____ at her desk and (listen) _____ to

the radio, too.

12. Jay (eat) _____ a grapefruit. He

(not, usually, eat) _____ them, but he

(want) _____ one today.

13. A: What (watch) _____ you _____?

B: *Spider-Man*.

A: Oh, I (like) _____ that movie.

14. Mark (play) _____ soccer every Saturday. Today is Saturday, but he

(not, play) _____. He (have) _____ a headache.

15. My brother Joey (have) _____ a new girlfriend. He

(like) _____ her a lot. They (watch) _____

a video at my house now.

16. A: I (love) _____ you.

B: I (love) _____ you, too.

17. A: What (do) _____ you _____ on Saturdays?

B: I (usually, go) _____ to the store,

(wash) _____ my car, and (read) _____ the

newspaper.

A: What (do) _____ you _____ now?

B: I (talk) _____ to you!

18. A: I (go) _____ to the store. (want) _____

you _____ anything?

B: We (need) _____ coffee.

A: I (not, like) _____ coffee.

B: Really? I (love) _____ it!

19. A: What (do) _____ your dad

_____?

B: He (fish) _____ with the girls.

A: Where?

B: They (be) _____ at the river.

I (see) _____ them.

Oh, they (have) _____ a fish!

A: (have) _____ they _____ a good time?

B: Yes, they (be) _____. The girls (smile)

_____ and Dad (look) _____ happy.

20. A: Look! (see) _____

you _____ those

girls?

B: Yes, I (do) _____.

They (be) _____ twins.

A: Where (live) _____

they _____?

B: Next door to me.

A: What (do) _____

they _____?

B: They (eat) _____ ice cream and

(smile) _____. They (also, look at) _____ us.

SELF-TEST

A Choose the best answer, A, B, C, or D, to complete the sentence. Mark your answer by darkening the oval with the same letter.

1. I _____ salad.

   A. am not liking   Ⓐ Ⓑ Ⓒ Ⓓ
   B. don't like
   C. am liking
   D. is liking

2. Pete _____ jeans today.

   A. is wearing   Ⓐ Ⓑ Ⓒ Ⓓ
   B. wears
   C. wearing
   D. am not wearing

3. The man _____ an umbrella.

   A. is hold   Ⓐ Ⓑ Ⓒ Ⓓ
   B. hold
   C. is holding
   D. aren't holding

4. Is the sun _____?

   A. shine   Ⓐ Ⓑ Ⓒ Ⓓ
   B. shining
   C. shines
   D. isn't shining

5. Sharon _____ the music.

   A. is hear   Ⓐ Ⓑ Ⓒ Ⓓ
   B. hear
   C. is hearing
   D. hears

6. _____ you like TV?

   A. Do   Ⓐ Ⓑ Ⓒ Ⓓ
   B. Is
   C. Are
   D. Does

7. Al _____ for the bus.

   A. is wait   Ⓐ Ⓑ Ⓒ Ⓓ
   B. wait
   C. are waiting
   D. is waiting

8. That girl _____ long hair.

   A. has   Ⓐ Ⓑ Ⓒ Ⓓ
   B. have
   C. is having
   D. are having

9. I _____ English.

   A. am liking   Ⓐ Ⓑ Ⓒ Ⓓ
   B. likes
   C. is liking
   D. like

10. _____ wash your car every week?

    A. Are you   Ⓐ Ⓑ Ⓒ Ⓓ
    B. Does you
    C. Do you
    D. Is you

B   Find the underlined word or phrase, A, B, C, or D, that is incorrect. Mark your answer by darkening the oval with the same letter.

1. I'm watch TV now.
   A B   C   D

   Ⓐ Ⓑ Ⓒ Ⓓ

2. The boys are playing in the park and the
      A   B
   girls is talking.
        C   D

   Ⓐ Ⓑ Ⓒ Ⓓ

3. It's Tuesday morning and I am sit in my
      A   B   C   D
   English class.

   Ⓐ Ⓑ Ⓒ Ⓓ

4. Soo Mi and Derek usually taking the bus
                     A   B   C
   in the morning.
        D

   Ⓐ Ⓑ Ⓒ Ⓓ

5. What are you doing? Do you studying?
          A   B   C   D

   Ⓐ Ⓑ Ⓒ Ⓓ

6. He isn't studying grammar every day.
      A   B   C   D

   Ⓐ Ⓑ Ⓒ Ⓓ

7. Henry's listen to music and doing
      A   B   C
   his homework.
        D

   Ⓐ Ⓑ Ⓒ Ⓓ

8. Are you know my parents?
      A   B   C   D

   Ⓐ Ⓑ Ⓒ Ⓓ

9. Do you liking Japanese food?
      A   B   C   D

   Ⓐ Ⓑ Ⓒ Ⓓ

10. I'm go to the store. Do you want anything?
      A B   C   D

   Ⓐ Ⓑ Ⓒ Ⓓ

UNIT 5
NOUNS AND PRONOUNS

5a Count and Noncount Nouns

Student Book p. 120

1 Practice

Write C next to the count nouns and N next to the noncount nouns.

1. __N__ gasoline
2. _____ help
3. _____ computer
4. _____ homework
5. _____ beauty
6. _____ backpack
7. _____ tomato
8. _____ luck
9. _____ apple
10. _____ music
11. _____ happiness

12. _____ water
13. _____ cake
14. _____ mail
15. _____ letter
16. _____ email
17. _____ student
18. _____ information
19. _____ furniture
20. _____ motorcycle
21. _____ peace
22. _____ tea

2 Practice

Write C next to the phrase if it is correct. Write I if it is incorrect.

__I__ 1. one rice
__C__ 2. one bed
_____ 3. one milk
_____ 4. one cheese
_____ 5. one flower

_____ 6. one mail
_____ 7. one homework
_____ 8. one window
_____ 9. one apple
_____ 10. one money

3 Practice

Think of things you can find in your kitchen. Then put them into two groups.

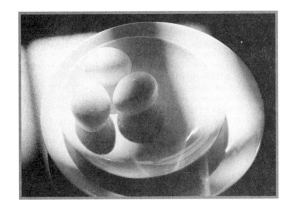

Count

1. _____eggs_____

2. _____

3. _____

4. _____

Noncount

5. _____rice_____

6. _____

7. _____

8. _____

5b *A, An,* and *Some*

Student Book p. 121

4 Practice

Paul and Linda are preparing for a dinner party. Here's a list of things they need. Complete with *a, an,* or *some*.

1	_____	coffee
2	_____	food
3	_____	table
4	_____	tablecloth
5	_____	cheese
6	_____	bread
7	_____	butter
8	_____	flowers
9	_____	stereo
10	_____	chairs

Nouns and Pronouns

5 Practice

What is in Theresa's kitchen? Complete the sentences with *a, an,* or *some*.

In Theresa's refrigerator, there are ___*some*___ eggs, _____ butter,
                                                1   2

and _____ block of cheese. Sometimes there is _____ bunch of
       3   4

grapes or _____ oranges. In her pantry, she usually has _____ jar
             5   6

of peanut butter, _____ loaf of bread, and _____ tea.
                 7   8

5c   *A, An,* or *The*

Student Book p. 123

6 Practice

Complete the sentences with *a, an,* or *the*.

A. It's ___*a*___ beautiful day. _____ weather is sunny. _____ sun is
       1   2   3

   shining. There's _____ park across the street. Children are in _____
                              4   5

   park. _____ children are riding bikes.
           6

B. There is _____ orange, _____ apple, and
               1   2

   _____ lemon on the table. _____ orange is
       3   4

   sweet, _____ apple is red, and _____ lemon
              5   6

   is sour.

C. Jack has _____ new house. _____ house has three bedrooms and
               1   2

   _____ kitchen. _____ kitchen is yellow and _____ bedrooms
       3   4   5

   are blue, white, and green.

D. A: What are you doing?

   B: I'm watching _____ movie.
                     1

   A: Do you want to come to the store with me?

   B: Yes, but I want to finish _____ movie first.
                                      2

E. A: How many children do you have?

   B: I have a girl and _____ boy.

                                               1

   A: How old are they?

   B: _____ girl is in high school, and _____ boy is working.

          2   3

F. My English class is fun. There's _____ student from Turkey and _____ student from Italy. _____ student from Turkey is an engineer in his country, and _____ student from Italy fixes cars. _____ class meets in _____ afternoon.

(blanks numbered 1–6)

G. My cousin Mary lives in _____ small town. _____ town has _____ library, _____ store, and _____ bank. Mary works at _____ bank.

(blanks numbered 1–6)

5d Generalizations

Student Book p. 125

7 Practice

Complete the sentences with *the* or *X* (no article).

1. A: Do you like __*X*__ music?

   B: I like __*the*__ music my brother plays, but I don't like _____ music my parents like.

2. Woo hoo! It's _____ last day of school!

3. Janice reads _____ magazines. _____ magazines on the table are interesting.

4. A: Where are you going?

   B: I'm going to _____ store. We need _____ fruit.

5. A: Do you like _____ sports?

   B: Not really.

6. A: Who is _____ girl in that photo?

   B: She's my cousin.

7. I like _____ animals. _____ cats are very soft. _____ dogs are big and friendly.

8. A: Do you like _____ Italian food?

    B: I love it. _____ food at *Luigi's* is very good.

9. A: I don't like _____ baseball.

    B: Really? I do. I'm watching _____ game right now!

10. Sarah loves _____ books. _____ book she's reading now is interesting.

5e   *Some* and *Any*

Student Book p. 126

8   Practice

Look at the photos and complete the sentences with *some* or *any*.

1. Is there _____ fruit?

2. Yes, there is _____ fruit.

3. Are there _____ dogs?

4. No, there aren't _____ dogs.

5. Are there _____ people on the street?

6. No, there aren't _____ people on the street.

7. Are there _____ tomatoes in the shop?

8. Yes, there are _____ tomatoes in the shop.

9. Is there _____ rice in the shop?

10. No, there isn't _____ rice in the shop.

11. Are there _____ people in the park?

12. Yes, there are _____ people in the park.

13. Are there _____ flowers in the park?

14. Yes, there are _____ flowers in the park.

15. Are there _____ birds in the photo?

16. No, there aren't _____ birds in the photo.

17. Are there _____ bicycles in the street?

18. No, there aren't _____ bicycles in the street.

19. Are there _____ people in the street?

20. Yes, there are _____ people in the street.

21. Are there _____ taxis in the street?

22. Yes, there are _____ taxis in the street.

Practice

Write *C* next to the sentence if *some* or *any* is used correctly. Write *I* if *some* or *any* is used incorrectly.

_____*I*_____ **1.** There aren't some eggs.

_____ **2.** There is some information.

_____ **3.** There aren't any telephones.

_____ **4.** Do you have some brothers or sisters?

_____ **5.** There isn't some money.

_____ **6.** Is there any bread?

_____ **7.** There isn't some butter.

_____ **8.** There aren't some napkins.

_____ **9.** There aren't any jobs here.

_____ **10.** Do you have any time?

5f ◆ Measurement Words

Student Book p. 128

10 Practice

Write the letter of any appropriate measurement word in front of each phrase. There may be more than one answer for each.

a. a bar of	**g.** a can of	**m.** a box of
b. a bunch of	**h.** a tube of	**n.** a glass of
c. a carton of	**i.** a sheet of	**o.** a bottle of
d. a piece of	**j.** a slice of	**p.** a cup of
e. a head of	**k.** a packet of	**q.** a roll of
f. a jar of	**l.** a loaf of	**r.** a bowl of

___*n, o, p, r*___ **1.** water

_____ **2.** soup

_____ **3.** spaghetti

_____ **4.** mayonnaise

_____ **5.** coffee

_____ **6.** toilet paper

_____ **7.** oil

_____ **8.** pizza

_____ **9.** bread

_____ **10.** cookies

_____ **11.** lettuce

_____ **12.** grapes

11 Practice

Write _C_ next to the phrase if the measurement words are correct. Write _I_ if the measurement words are incorrect.

_____I_____ **1.** a loaf of milk

_____ **2.** a jar of toilet paper

_____ **3.** a bowl of soup

_____ **4.** a head of lettuce

_____ **5.** a can of paper

_____ **6.** a piece of toothpaste

_____ **7.** a packet of spaghetti

_____ **8.** a bottle of water

_____ **9.** a tube of lettuce

_____ **10.** a carton of milk

12 Practice

Do you need to go to the store? Write sentences using measurement words.

1. _I need two bars of soap_____.

2. _____.

3. _____.

4. _____.

5. _____.

6. _____.

7. _____.

8. _____.

9. _____.

10. _____.

5g Quantifying Expressions

Student Book p. 130

13 Practice

Complete the sentences with *much* or *many*.

1. Karl doesn't eat _____ *much* _____ candy.

2. He doesn't drink _____ wine.

3. He likes _____ kinds of movies.

4. He doesn't spend _____ time on housework.

5. He doesn't get _____ exercise.

6. He likes _____ kinds of cheese.

7. He has _____ friends.

8. He doesn't have _____ money.

9. He drinks _____ cups of coffee every day.

10. He doesn't have _____ problems.

14 Practice

Complete the sentences with *a few* or *a little*.

1. Kathy has _____ *a little* _____ butter on her bread.

2. She eats _____ fruit in the morning.

3. She has _____ flowers in her garden.

4. She talks on the phone for _____ hours.

5. She listens to _____ music at night.

6. She has _____ brothers.

7. She eats _____ fish every week.

8. She drinks _____ wine.

9. She puts _____ milk in her tea.

10. She has _____ parties in the summer.

15 Practice

How much do you use, eat, drink, or have of these things? Write sentences using *a lot of*, *not much*, **or** *not many*.

cereal	eggs	homework	money	sugar
cookies	friends	milk	problems	toothpaste

1. *I don't use much toothpaste* .
2. _____ .
3. _____ .
4. _____ .
5. _____ .
6. _____ .
7. _____ .
8. _____ .
9. _____ .
10. _____ .

16 Practice

Write *C* **next to the sentence if** *much, many, a little,* **or** *a few* **is used correctly.
Write** *I* **if** *much, many, a little,* **or** *a few* **is used incorrectly.**

_C_ **1.** There isn't much coffee.

_I_ **2.** I have much apples.

_____ **3.** There is a little ice cream.

_____ **4.** There isn't many rice.

_____ **5.** They don't have much money.

_____ **6.** She has a few time.

_____ **7.** We don't have many salt and pepper.

_____ **8.** He doesn't eat much meat.

_____ **9.** We need a few potatoes.

_____ **10.** We need a little rain.

17 **Practice**

Read about Mary and Bill's family. First write questions with *how much* and *how many*. Then write answers to them.

Mary and Bill have two children. Mary's brother and his two children also live with them. Mary and Bill buy a lot of food every week. They buy two jars of peanut butter, two large containers of yogurt, six pounds of vegetables, two cartons of eggs, four loaves of bread, a lot of butter, a lot of rice, a little ice cream, a lot of fruit, three bottles of juice, a little meat, a little cheese, and a few potatoes.

1. (yogurt) _How much yogurt do they buy_ ?

   They buy two large containers of yogurt .

2. (eggs) _____ ?

   _____ .

3. (vegetables) _____ ?

   _____ .

4. (peanut butter) _____ ?

   _____ .

5. (bread) _____ ?

   _____ .

6. (butter) _____?

_____.

7. (rice) _____?

_____.

8. (potatoes) _____?

_____.

9. (meat) _____?

_____.

10. (fruit) _____?

_____.

11. (ice cream) _____?

_____.

12. (food) _____?

_____.

|8| Practice

Write questions and answers with *how much* and *how many*.

1. big problems/you/have

How many big problems do you have _____?

I don't have any big problems _____.

2. hours/you/spend/on the computer

_____?

_____.

3. parties/you/go to/every month

_____?

_____.

4. homework/you/have/every day

_____?

_____.

5. furniture/you/have/in your room

_____?

_____.

6. ice cream/you/eat/every month

_____?

_____.

7. coffee/you/drink/every day

_____?

_____.

8. books/you/read/in a year

_____?

_____.

5i *Whose* and Possessive Nouns

Student Book p. 134

19 Practice

Answer the questions using the words in parentheses. Put the apostrophe in the correct place.

1. Whose skates are these? (the girls)

_Those are the girls' skates_____.

2. Whose clothes are those? (the women)

_____.

3. Whose scarf is this? (Jody)

_____.

4. Whose sandwich is that? (Peter)

_____.

5. Whose backpacks are these? (the men)

_____.

6. Whose dog is this? (the children)

_____.

7. Whose car is that? (Mike)

_____.

8. Whose shoes are those? (Carole)

_____.

20 Practice

Underline _whose_ or _who's_ to complete each question.

1. (Whose / Who's) the girl in the photo?

2. (Whose / Who's) photo is that?

3. (Whose / Who's) bag is in the bedroom?

4. (Whose / Who's) in the bedroom?

5. (Whose / Who's) coming to the party?

6. (Whose / Who's) party are we going to?

21 Practice

Add ' (apostrophe) or 's to show possession.

1. Every Friday night I go to my friend Cindy house.

2. Cindy house is on a quiet street.

3. She has two cats and a dog. The dog name is Archie.

4. The cats names are Sammy and Jackson.

5. We take Cindy car to the restaurant.

6. Sometimes we meet our friends. Our friends names are Kathy and Sally.

SELF-TEST

A **Choose the best answer, A, B, C, or D, to complete the sentence. Mark your answer by darkening the oval with the same letter.**

1. I live in _____ apartment.

   A. a   Ⓐ Ⓑ Ⓒ Ⓓ
   B. an
   C. the
   D. any

2. There isn't _____ noise.

   A. a few   Ⓐ Ⓑ Ⓒ Ⓓ
   B. some
   C. many
   D. any

3. I need a _____ of bananas.

   A. loaf   Ⓐ Ⓑ Ⓒ Ⓓ
   B. bunch
   C. bottle
   D. roll

4. _____ dog is that?

   A. Who's   Ⓐ Ⓑ Ⓒ Ⓓ
   B. How many
   C. Whose
   D. How much

5. I need _____ money.

   A. some   Ⓐ Ⓑ Ⓒ Ⓓ
   B. any
   C. much
   D. many

6. How _____ children does he have?

   A. some   Ⓐ Ⓑ Ⓒ Ⓓ
   B. any
   C. much
   D. many

7. She needs _____ eggs.

   A. a few   Ⓐ Ⓑ Ⓒ Ⓓ
   B. a little
   C. any
   D. many

8. Those are the _____ hats.

   A. womens'   Ⓐ Ⓑ Ⓒ Ⓓ
   B. woman
   C. womens
   D. women's

9. _____ is interesting.

   A. The history   Ⓐ Ⓑ Ⓒ Ⓓ
   B. An history
   C. History
   D. A history

10. That's _____ cat.

    A. Kathy'   Ⓐ Ⓑ Ⓒ Ⓓ
    B. Kathy's
    C. Kathys'
    D. Kathys

B **Find the underlined word or phrase, A, B, C, or D, that is incorrect. Mark your answer by darkening the oval with the same letter.**

1. I need two carton of milk from the store.
   A   B   C   D

   Ⓐ Ⓑ Ⓒ Ⓓ

2. I don't have much time or many money.
   A   B   C   D

   Ⓐ Ⓑ Ⓒ Ⓓ

3. There isn't some information
   A   B   C
   in the newspaper.
   D

   Ⓐ Ⓑ Ⓒ Ⓓ

4. Who's children are they?
   A   B   C   D

   Ⓐ Ⓑ Ⓒ Ⓓ

5. I don't have some cheese or juice.
   A   B   C   D

   Ⓐ Ⓑ Ⓒ Ⓓ

6. He drinks a little glasses of water
              A   B   C
   every day.
   D

   Ⓐ Ⓑ Ⓒ Ⓓ

7. How much backpacks are there
   A   B   C
   in the boys' room?
   D

   Ⓐ Ⓑ Ⓒ Ⓓ

8. My mother name is Peg, and my
      A   B
   father's name is Bob.
   C   D

   Ⓐ Ⓑ Ⓒ Ⓓ

9. Whose the boy in the kitchen with you?
   A   B   C   D

   Ⓐ Ⓑ Ⓒ Ⓓ

10. I like the history. It's a good subject.
    A   B   C   D

   Ⓐ Ⓑ Ⓒ Ⓓ

UNIT 6
THE SIMPLE PAST TENSE

6a The Simple Past Tense: Regular Verbs
Student Book p. 142

1 Practice
Complete the sentences with the simple past tense of the verbs in parentheses.

Mark (stay) _____ home yesterday. He (watch) _____
    1   2
TV and (listen) _____ to the radio. He (work) _____ in the
        3   4
garden and (clean) _____ the house. He (wash) _____
              5   6
clothes and (play) _____ games on his computer. He
              7
(shop) _____ and (cook) _____ dinner. When his wife
        8   9
(finish) _____ working, she (kiss) _____ him.
          10   11

2 Practice
Write sentences about your day yesterday. Use verbs from the list or add your own.

brush	cook	play	talk	wash
clean	finish	start	walk	work

1. *Yesterday, I washed my clothes* _____.

2. _____.

3. _____.

4. _____.

5. _____.

6. _____.

7. _____.

8. _____.

3 Practice
Complete the sentences with simple present or the simple past of the verbs in parentheses.

1. Two years ago, Elizabeth (work) _____ *worked* _____ for an Internet company.

2. Now, she (work) _____ in a restaurant.

3. Every day, customers (order) _____ lunch and dinner.

4. Usually, she (like) _____ her job.

5. And she (make) _____ good money.

6. But yesterday, a customer (change) _____ his order three times.

7. Usually, she (finish) _____ work at 9:00.

8. Yesterday, she (work) _____ until 11:00.

4 Practice

Write C next to the sentence if the verb is correct. Write I if the verb is incorrect.

_C_   **1.** Sheila walks to school every day.

_I_   **2.** Sheila walks to school last week.

_____   **3.** She took the bus every night.

_____   **4.** She eats lunch with her sister on Sundays.

_____   **5.** Two years ago, she works at a restaurant.

_____   **6.** Now, she works at home.

_____   **7.** Now, Tom talked to his mother.

_____   **8.** Yesterday, he talked to his brother.

_____   **9.** Yesterday, he listens to music.

_____ **10.** He likes music.

6b Past Time Expressions

Student Book p. 145

5 Practice

Complete the conversations with *yesterday*, *last*, or *ago*.

A. Lisa: What happened? I waited two hours for you _____*yesterday*_____ .
                                                                    1

       Maggie: I know. I'm sorry. My mother called _____
                                                                           2

                afternoon because she needed my help. I walked back to my house and only

                arrived home about two hours _____ .
                                                                      3

B. _____, I worked from 9:00 until 5:00. I worked six days
        1

_____ week. I worked six days a week _____
    2   3

month. I need a vacation!

C. Leslie finished school ten years _____. _____
                                                       1   2

year, she started a new job. _____ week, she moved to a new
                                             3

apartment. I visited her _____.
                                      4

D. _____ week, my boss asked me to write his report. Three days
        1

_____, he asked me to make coffee. _____, he
    2   3

wanted me to buy his wife a present. Today, I told him that I quit!

6   Practice

Use time expressions to complete the sentences about yourself.

1. Six months ago, _I moved to Boston_____.

2. Last month, _____.

3. Last week, _____.

4. Yesterday afternoon, _____.

5. One year ago, _____.

6. Three hours ago, _____.

6c   Spelling of Regular Past Tense Verbs

Student Book p. 148

7   Practice

Write the correct spelling of the simple past tense form.

Base Verb	Past Tense		Base Verb	Past Tense
1. plan	_planned_		5. refer	_____
2. enjoy	_____		6. hug	_____
3. dance	_____		7. pass	_____
4. lie	_____		8. paint	_____

Base Verb	Past Tense		Base Verb	Past Tense
9. cry	_____		**12.** occur	_____
10. play	_____		**13.** decide	_____
11. try	_____		**14.** look	_____

8 Practice

Circle the correct form of the verbs in parentheses.

1. We (tried / tryed) the new restaurant.

2. He (lied / lyed) about his age.

3. Rebecca (decided / decideed) to go shopping.

4. Jason (prefered / preferred) to stay home.

5. David (stoped / stopped) at the red light.

6. The baby (cryed / cried) all night.

7. The boys (studyed / studied) in the afternoon.

8. My father (walkd / walked) five miles to school.

9. My mother (huged / hugged) me at the airport.

10. Robert (fixed / fixxed) the car.

11. They (planed / planned) a surprise for her.

12. Juan (visited / visitted) the library.

13. Sharon (cookked / cooked) dinner.

14. Mark (carryed / carried) the bags.

15. We (enjoied / enjoyed) the party.

16. We (played / plaied) music for four hours.

9 Practice

Look at the reading and complete the sentences. Use the simple past of verbs from the list.

continue	jump
dance	marry
die	rain
drop	smile
finish	start

This is a picture of my grandparents' wedding. They _____ in 1952.

1

My grandmother is alive, but my grandfather _____ five years ago. Look

2

at the picture. It _____ that day, but they just _____

3   4

at the camera. They were very happy. This is a funny story. After the wedding, the

reception _____ at 2:00 and _____ at 4:00. Everyone

5   6

_____ because the music was good. But the cake was on a small table.

7

At one point, everyone _____ up and down at the same time and the

8

cake _____ to the floor! But it was okay. They _____

9   10

having a good time.

10 Practice

Write sentences about your last vacation.

1. _We visited London last summer_____.

2. _____.

3. _____.

4. _____.

5. _____.

6. _____.

6d Pronunciation of -ed: /t/, /d/, and /id/

Student Book p. 154

II Practice

Complete the sentences with the simple past tense of the verbs. Then read the sentences aloud and check the column for the pronunciation of each verb.

Alex is ten years old. Yesterday, he (start) ___*started*___ his day with some fruit
₁

and juice for breakfast. He (walk) _____ to school and (study) _____
₂   ₃

all day. At 4:00, he (finish) _____ his homework. He (call) _____ his
₄   ₅

friend, John. He (invite) _____ John to his house. The two boys (play)
₆

_____ for two hours. Alex (want) _____ John to spend the night.
₇   ₈

John (ask) _____ his mother, and his mom (allow) _____ him to
₉   ₁₀

stay. The boys (watch) _____ TV and (talk) _____ until 11:00. They
₁₁   ₁₂

(try) _____ to sleep outside, but it (start) _____ to rain.
₁₃   ₁₄

	/t/	/d/	/id/
1. start	_____	_____	_X_
2. walk	_____	_____	_____
3. study	_____	_____	_____
4. finish	_____	_____	_____
5. call	_____	_____	_____
6. invite	_____	_____	_____
7. play	_____	_____	_____
8. want	_____	_____	_____
9. ask	_____	_____	_____
10. allow	_____	_____	_____
11. watch	_____	_____	_____
12. talk	_____	_____	_____
13. try	_____	_____	_____
14. start	_____	_____	_____

12 Practice

Complete the sentences with the past tense of verbs from the list. Then circle the final *-ed* sound.

arrive	decide	listen	start	wait	work
brush	finish	plan	turn	wash	yawn

Jane _____*yawned*_____ (t / d / id) and _____ (t / d / id)
          1   2

off the alarm. She _____ (t / d / id) her face and
                               3

_____ (t / d / id) her teeth. She _____ (t / d / id) to
          4   5

the news and _____ (t / d / id) her day. She _____
                   6   7

(t / d / id) for the bus, but it was late. Jane _____ (t / d / id) to ride
                                                  8

her bicycle. She _____ (t / d / id) at her job and
                        9

_____ (t / d / id) for eight hours. At 6:00, Jane
     10

_____ (t / d / id) and _____ (t / d / id) to go home.
     11   12

6e The Simple Past Tense: Irregular Verbs

Student Book p. 156

13 Practice

Complete the sentences with the past tense irregular verbs.

A. Yesterday (be) _____*was*_____ Josh's birthday. He (go) _____
          1   2

to the store and (buy) _____ some meat, onions, and wine. He
                             3

(come) _____ home and (make) _____ dinner for
          4   5

his friends. His friends (give) _____ him a present, a new puppy!
                                     6

They (eat) _____ and (drink) _____ a lot. Everyone
          7   8

(have) _____ a really good time!
         9

B. Elena (meet) _____ Ernesto 20 years ago. They (become)
                  1

_____very good friends and (get) _____ married
     2   3

in 1984. Back then, Ernesto (teach) _____ high school, and Elena
                                     4

(take) _____ classes at the university.
     5

C. I'm so tired! I (get) _____ up at 2:00 last night. I (read)
1
_____ a magazine and (sit) _____ on the sofa. I
2   3
(drink) _____ some warm milk. Finally, I (go) _____
4   5
to bed and (sleep) _____ for four hours.
6

14 Practice

Write *C* next to the sentence if the past tense of the verb is correct. Write *I* if the past tense of the verb is incorrect.

I   **1.** Yesterday, we buyed some milk and bananas.

C   **2.** We went to the store.

_____   **3.** It started to rain an hour ago.

_____   **4.** We heard the news this morning.

_____   **5.** They eated French bread for breakfast.

_____   **6.** Janet drank some coffee.

_____   **7.** I told him the time.

_____   **8.** You had a good time last night.

_____   **9.** We seed him last week.

_____   **10.** Jack visited Cindy on vacation.

15 Practice

Complete the sentences about Buzz Aldrin, the astronaut. Write the correct form of the verbs in parentheses. Use the simple present or the simple past.

Buzz Aldrin was born in Montclair, New Jersey in 1930.

He (attend) ___*attended*___ West Point. He
1

(become) _____ a pilot and (fly)
2

_____ many kinds of planes. He (get)
3

_____ his doctorate in 1963. That year,
4

NASA (National Aeronautic and Space Administration)

(choose) _____ him to be one of the
5

first astronauts.

In July 1969, Buzz Aldrin and Neil Armstrong (become) _____ the
———
6

first people to walk on the moon. Thousands of people around the world (watch)

_____ this on TV.
———
7

In 1988, he (marry) _____ Lois Driggs. They (have)
———
8

_____ six children now and (enjoy) _____ skiing in
———   ———
9   10

their free time.

In 1993, Aldrin (start) _____ his own company. He (call)
———
11

_____ the company "Starcraft Boosters". Today, he (travel)
———
12

_____ around the country and (talk) _____ about the
———   ———
13   14

future of space exploration.

16 Practice

Write sentences about yourself. Use verbs from the list or your own. Use the simple present, the present progressive, or the simple past.

be	go	listen	ride a bicycle	study	travel
drive	have	play	stay	take a nap	work

1. Last year, I _was on a soccer team_____.

2. Six months ago, I _____.

3. Two weeks ago, I _____.

4. Yesterday, I _____.

5. On Saturdays, I _____.

6. I usually _____.

7. I never _____.

8. Right now, I _____.

9. Now, my mom _____.

10. And my best friend _____.

6f ◆ The Simple Past Tense: Negative

Student Book p. 161

17 Practice

Read the following affirmative and negative simple present tense sentences. Change the verbs to the simple past tense.

1. I don't clean every day.

   I _____ *didn't clean* _____ yesterday.

2. I don't have a cell phone.

   Last summer, I _____.

3. Jane teaches history.

   She _____ last semester.

4. My father flies an airplane.

   Last month, my father _____.

5. I don't eat breakfast.

   This morning, I _____.

6. You don't go to the gym.

   You _____ yesterday morning.

7. I'm not tired.

   I _____ last night.

8. We go skiing every winter.

   Last winter, we _____.

9. Lupe doesn't smoke.

   She _____ five years ago.

10. My brother doesn't watch TV.

    Last night, he _____.

11. They aren't in my class.

    Three days ago, they _____.

12. I drink some milk.

    I _____ an hour ago.

Practice

Cathy and Tina are roommates. Read each sentence about their day yesterday. First, provide the past tense of the verb in parentheses. Then complete the sentence with the negative form.

1. Cathy (get) _got_ up early, but Tina _____ *didn't get up early* _____ .

2. Tina (eat) _____ breakfast, but _____

   _____ .

3. Cathy (go) _____ to class, but _____

   _____ .

4. Cathy (study) _____ for the test, but _____

   _____ .

5. Tina (call) _____ her mother, but _____

   _____ .

6. Cathy (feel) _____ good, but _____

   _____ .

7. Tina (buy) _____ lunch, but _____

   _____ .

8. Tina (do) _____ her homework, but _____

   _____ .

9. Cathy (make) _____ dinner, but _____

   _____ .

10. Tina (have) _____ a headache, but _____

   _____ .

19 Practice

Write sentences about what you didn't do when you were a child and what you do now. Use verbs from the list or add your own.

buy	drink	eat	shop	wear
do homework	drive	play video games	smoke	work

1. _When I was a child, I didn't even eat green beans, but I eat them now_ .

2. _____ .

3. _____ .

4. _____ .

5. _____ .

6. _____ .

7. _____ .

8. _____ .

9. _____ .

10. _____ .

20 Practice

Write affirmative and negative statements.

1. Picasso/ paint/ *Mona Lisa*

   Picasso didn't paint the Mona Lisa. .

2. Henry Ford/ invent/ the lightbulb

   _____ .

3. George Lucas/ direct/ *Star Wars*

   _____ .

4. Shakespeare/ write/ *Harry Potter*

   _____ .

5. Jennifer Lopez/ play/ Selena, the Mexican pop star

   _____ .

6. Madonna/ sing/ *La Vida Loca*

   _____ .

7. Beethoven/ compose/ *The Ninth Symphony*

   _____ .

21   **Practice**

Complete the conversations using the simple past tense of the verbs in parentheses.

A. Sheryl: (play) _____ you _____ sports in high
                    1   (1)
            school?

Lynn: No, _____ .
                     2

Sheryl: (have) _____ you _____ a lot of friends
                    3   (3)
            in high school?

Lynn: No, _____ .
                     4

Sheryl: (study) _____ you _____ a lot in high
                    5   (5)
            school?

Lynn: Yes, _____ .
                     6

B. Bill: (go) _____ Beth _____ to school
                1   (1)
          yesterday?

Ann: No, _____ .
                 2

Bill: (clean) _____ she _____ her bedroom?
               3   (3)

Ann: No, _____ .
                 4

Bill: (do) _____ she _____ anything?
             5   (5)

Ann: No, _____ . She (have) _____ a headache.
                6   7

C. Debbie: (go) _____ you _____ out with Mark
                1   (1)
           last night?

Irene: Yes, _____ . We (go) _____ to a movie.
                2   3

Debbie: (have) _____ you _____ a good time?
                4   (4)

Irene: Yes, _____ .
                     5

Practice

Write questions and answers about what you did last weekend.

1. you/ go away

   Did you go away last weekend _____?

   No, I didn't. I stayed at home _____.

2. you/ play baseball

   _____?

   _____.

3. you/ see a movie

   _____?

   _____.

4. you/ read the newspaper

   _____?

   _____.

5. you/ go dancing

   _____?

   _____.

6. you/ eat pizza

   _____?

   _____.

7. you/ drink soda

   _____?

   _____.

8. you/ buy groceries

   _____?

   _____.

The Simple Past Tense: Wh- Questions

Student Book p. 167

23 **Practice**

Match the questions with the answers.

_c_ **1.** What did you do Friday night?   **a.** At 10:30.

____ **2.** What did you see?   **b.** It was good.

____ **3.** Who did you go with?   **c.** I went to a movie.

____ **4.** How was it?   **d.** Charlie.

____ **5.** When did it end?   **e.** That new love story.

24 **Practice**

Write questions and answers using the following prompts.

A. Jane: what/you/do/Friday night

What did you do Friday night _____?

Peggy: we/go/party

We went to a party _____.

Jane: who/see/there

_____?

Peggy: we/see/Rita and Joe

_____.

Jane: how/they/look

_____?

Peggy: they/look/fine

_____.

Jane: when/they/arrive/in town

_____?

Peggy: they/arrive/two days ago

_____.

Jane: when/you/get home

_____?

Peggy: we/get/home/at 1:00

_____.

B. Janine: what/you/do/last night

_____?

Paul: we/go/movie

_____.

Janine: who/you/go/with

_____?

Paul: I/go/with/Frank

_____.

Janine: how/you/go the theater

_____?

Paul: we/take/the bus

_____.

Janine: when/you/get home

_____?

Paul: we/get home/at 4:00

_____.

The Simple Past Tense

C. Nancy: what/you/buy

_____?

Karen: I/buy/a magazine

_____.

Nancy: why/you/buy/it

_____?

Karen: I/like/the photos

_____.

Nancy: where/you/find/it

_____?

Karen: I/find/it/at the drugstore

_____.

6i The Simple Past Tense: Time Clauses with *Before* and *After*
Student Book p. 172

25 Practice
Underline the time clauses in the sentences. Circle the main clauses.

1. After Kelly went to the store, she worked on her computer.

2. Before she made dinner, she worked out.

3. She watched the news before she took a shower.

4. Before she listened to music, she called her mother.

5. After she did the dishes, she read the newspaper.

6. She went to bed after she brushed her teeth.

26 Practice

Combine the two sentences. Write as many sentences using *after* and *before* as you can. Note that there are two possible sentences for *after* and two for *before*.

1. Trisha went to college. She got a job.

   (before) _Trisha went to college before she got a job._

   Before she got a job, Trisha went to college.

   (after) _After she went to college, Trisha got a job._

   Trisha got a job after she went to college.

2. We bought tickets. We went on vacation.

   (before) _____

   _____

   (after) _____

   _____

3. The Thompsons bought a new camera. They took photos.

   (before) _____

   _____

   (after) _____

   _____

4. He went to the store. He made dinner.

   (before) _____

   _____

   (after) _____

   _____

5. Renee bought a new dress. She went to the party.

   (before) _____

   _____

   (after) _____

   _____

6. I had a toothache. I went to the dentist.

(before) _____

_____

(after) _____

_____

7. Derek studied very hard. He took the test.

(before) _____

_____

(after) _____

_____

8. Buffy and Anya finished high school. They traveled around Europe.

(before) _____

_____

(after) _____

_____

9. Jane learned to play the guitar. She joined a band.

(before) _____

_____

(after) _____

_____

10. Ron worked out. He took a shower.

(before) _____

_____

(after) _____

_____

A Choose the best answer, A, B, C, or D, to complete the sentence. Mark your answer by darkening the oval with the same letter.

1. How many children _____?

   A. she had   Ⓐ Ⓑ Ⓒ Ⓓ
   B. did she had
   C. did she
   D. did she have

2. They _____ a trip to Vietnam three years ago.

   A. took   Ⓐ Ⓑ Ⓒ Ⓓ
   B. take
   C. taked
   D. takes

3. Fifty years _____, people didn't play computer games.

   A. yesterday   Ⓐ Ⓑ Ⓒ Ⓓ
   B. ago
   C. now
   D. last

4. People _____ microwaves fifty years ago.

   A. didn't use   Ⓐ Ⓑ Ⓒ Ⓓ
   B. use
   C. didn't used
   D. didn't

5. When did you _____ home?

   A. get   Ⓐ Ⓑ Ⓒ Ⓓ
   B. got
   C. did
   D. didn't get

6. _____ week, Ben taught his first class.

   A. Yesterday   Ⓐ Ⓑ Ⓒ Ⓓ
   B. Ago
   C. Now
   D. Last

7. Where were you? I called you ten minutes _____.

   A. yesterday   Ⓐ Ⓑ Ⓒ Ⓓ
   B. ago
   C. now
   D. last

8. Why _____ to class?

   A. you came   Ⓐ Ⓑ Ⓒ Ⓓ
   B. didn't you come
   C. didn't you came
   D. didn't come

9. He took a shower _____ he went to the party.

   A. before   Ⓐ Ⓑ Ⓒ Ⓓ
   B. ago
   C. yesterday
   D. last

10. A: Vicky, did you enjoy your vacation?
    B: _____.

    A. No, I did   Ⓐ Ⓑ Ⓒ Ⓓ
    B. Yes, I didn't
    C. No, I didn't
    D. Yes, I enjoyed

B   Find the underlined word or phrase, A, B, C, or D, that is incorrect. Mark your answer by darkening the oval with the same letter.

1. Jack <u>went</u> to the store, <u>bought</u> <u>some food</u>,
       A   B   C

   and <u>make</u> dinner for his friends.
       D

   Ⓐ Ⓑ Ⓒ Ⓓ

2. <u>Ago week</u>, my mother <u>had</u>
     A   B

   <u>a doctor's appointment</u>
          C

   <u>at 10:30 in the morning</u>.
          D

   Ⓐ Ⓑ Ⓒ Ⓓ

3. Chelsea and Nathan <u>drinked</u> soda and <u>ate</u>
                      A   B

   pizza <u>before</u> they <u>went</u> to the movie.
         C   D

   Ⓐ Ⓑ Ⓒ Ⓓ

4. We <u>watched</u> TV <u>last night</u>. We <u>didn't went</u>
      A   B   C

   to a movie, but we <u>ordered</u> a pizza.
                   D

   Ⓐ Ⓑ Ⓒ Ⓓ

5. My father <u>didn't speak</u> English <u>before</u> he
             A   B

   <u>come</u> <u>to this country</u>.
     C   D

   Ⓐ Ⓑ Ⓒ Ⓓ

6. <u>Did you</u> <u>take the bus</u>, or <u>did you rode</u>
     A   B   C

   your bike <u>yesterday</u>?
           D

   Ⓐ Ⓑ Ⓒ Ⓓ

7. We <u>get dressed</u>, <u>went to the store</u>,
       A   B

   <u>bought some fruit</u>, and
        C

   <u>drank a glass of juice</u>.
        D

   Ⓐ Ⓑ Ⓒ Ⓓ

8. <u>Who</u> <u>did you see</u> <u>at the party</u> <u>ago night</u>?
    A   B   C   D

   Ⓐ Ⓑ Ⓒ Ⓓ

9. I <u>wanted</u> to be <u>a doctor</u>, but <u>I didn't</u>
     A   B   C

   <u>studied</u>.
     D

   Ⓐ Ⓑ Ⓒ Ⓓ

10. My class <u>finished</u> the exercise <u>before</u> my
           A   B

    teacher <u>return</u> to the room <u>last week</u>.
          C   D

    Ⓐ Ⓑ Ⓒ Ⓓ

UNIT 7
THE PAST PROGRESSIVE TENSE

7a The Past Progressive Tense
Student Book p.180

1 Practice
Read the following sentences. Change the verbs to the past progressive tense.

1. I am watching TV now.

   Yesterday at this time, I _____*was watching*_____ TV.

2. They are not doing their homework now.

   Yesterday at this time, they _____*weren't doing*_____ their homework.

3. My mother is sending email now.

   Yesterday at this time, she _____ email.

4. My brothers are playing music.

   Yesterday at this time, they _____ music.

5. Mike isn't using the computer.

   Yesterday at this time, Mike _____ the computer.

6. They aren't cleaning the house.

   Yesterday at this time, they _____ the house.

7. She is reading.

   Yesterday at this time, she _____ .

8. I am not talking on the phone.

   Yesterday at this time, I _____ on the phone.

9. Dave and Frank are researching whales online.

   Yesterday at this time, they _____ whales online.

10. Erik is swimming now.

    Yesterday at this time, he _____ .

11. My sister isn't riding her motorcycle.

    Yesterday at this time, she _____ her motorcycle.

12. They aren't playing video games.

Yesterday at this time, they _____ video games.

Practice

What was happening last Saturday? Write questions and answers about the photos using the past progressive tense.

1. Marilyn/pour/juice

A: _What was Marilyn doing_ ?

B: _She was pouring juice_ .

2. Paul and Jay/play/dog

A: _____ ?

B: _____ .

3. they/go/to library

A: _____ ?

B: _____ .

4. the family/relax/at home

A: _____ ?

B: _____ .

5. Gloria/do/laundry

A: _____ ?

B: _____ .

6. we/paint/the wall

A: _____ ?

B: _____ .

3 Practice

Write questions and answers about your activities.

1. last night at 7:00   _What were you doing at 7:00 last night_ ?

    I was watching TV   .

2. at 8:30 this morning   _____?

    _____.

3. this time last year   _____?

    _____.

4. 30 minutes ago   _____?

    _____.

5. last Saturday afternoon _____?

    _____.

6. this time last week   _____?

    _____.

7. at midnight last night _____?

    _____.

4 Practice

Answer the questions with a negative past progressive verb. Then add a statement using the prompt in parentheses.

1. Were Kathy and Josh driving to work this morning?

    No, _they weren't driving to work. They were taking the bus_.
    (take the bus)

2. Was it raining when you left the house?

    No, _____. (snow)

3. Were you doing your homework when I called?

    No, _____. (play video games)

4. Was she sleeping?

    No, _____. (take a shower)

5. Were the children crying?

    No, _____. (laugh)

6. Was Mr. Yashita shopping?

No, _____. (just look)

7. Was he walking to school at 7:00?

No, _____. (ride his bicycle)

8. Were you taking photos of the new building?

No, we _____. (talk about)

9. Were they listening to the radio?

No, _____. (play guitar)

10. Was she looking at me?

No, _____. (look at me)

7b *While* and *When* with Past Time Clauses

Student Book p. 185

5 | Practice

Write as many sentences as you can using *when* or *while* and the past progressive or simple past.

1. sun/shine/I/leave my house

The sun was shining when I left my house. When I left my house, the sun was shining .

2. I/dream/alarm/ring

I was dreaming when the alarm rang. When the alarm rang, I was dreaming. While I was dreaming, the alarm rang .
The alarm rang while I was dreaming .

3. Steve/read/teacher/call on him

_____

_____

4. it/rain/I/arrive at work

_____

_____

5. Roger/snowboard/he/fall

_____

_____

6. I/not, smile/he/take my photo

_____

_____

7. I/drive/my car/have a problem

_____

_____

8. I/work/at a restaurant/I/meet/my husband

_____

_____

9. Shannon/look at the map/she/find/the city

_____

_____

10. I/think about/you/you/call/me

_____

_____

| 6 | Practice

Complete the sentences with the simple past or the past progressive of the verbs in parentheses.

A. I (sit) _____ at home when the doorbell (ring) _____. When I
                    1   2
(open) _____ it, a man (stand) _____ there. I
              3   4
(not, know) _____ him. He (sell) _____ magazines.
                    5   6

B. My friend Mike (have) _____ a party last Friday night. A lot of people
                                    1
(be) _____ there. When I (get) _____ there, they
            2   3
(dance) _____ and (laugh) _____, and Mike (eat) _____.
              4   5   6
We (play) _____ music loudly when a neighbor (come) _____ and
                  7   8

(ask) _____ Mike to turn it down. He (turn) _____ down the
            9   10
music, and everyone (leave) _____ around 1:00. It (be) _____ a
                                    11   12
good party!

C. My parents (have) _____ a surprise yesterday. They (go) _____ to
                            1   2
a restaurant. When they (finish) _____ dinner, my father
                                        3
(take) _____ out his wallet. He (not, have) _____ any money!
            4   5

7c The Past Progressive Tense and the Simple Past Tense
Student Book p. 187

7 Practice

Complete the sentences with the simple past or past progressive of the verbs in parentheses.

A. A: How (be) _____ your vacation?
                        1

B: It (be) _____ great. A week ago, we (ski) _____ and
                2   3
(hike) _____. I also (ask) _____ my girlfriend to marry me.
            4   5

A: Really?

B: Yes, we (eat) _____ dinner at a small romantic restaurant when I
                        6
(take) _____ out the ring from my coat.
            7

A: What (say) _____ she _____?
                    8   (8)

B: She (say) _____, "Yes!"
                    9

A: Congratulations!

B. Eva (shop) _____ yesterday when she (see) _____
                              1   **2**

some pretty shoes. She (go) _____ in the store,
                                            3

(try) _____ them on, and (buy) _____ them.
                    4   **5**

C. A: Where (be) _____ you this morning? I
                            1

    (call) _____ , but you (not, answer) _____ .
                          2   **3**

    B: I (play) _____ with my family in the park. We (sit) _____
                        4   **5**

    and (laugh) _____ . It (be) _____ a beautiful morning.
                      6   **7**

    The sun (shine) _____ and, it (not, be) _____ cold.
                            8   **9**

D. I (have) _____ an interesting day yesterday. While I (wait)
                1

_____ for the bus, I (meet) _____ a friendly man at the bus
        2   **3**

stop. We (start) _____ talking. When the bus (come) _____ ,
                      4   **5**

we (get on) _____ . When I (get off) _____ the bus, I (pick
                    6   **7**

up) _____ my briefcase and (say) _____ goodbye to the
              8   **9**

man. I (arrive) _____ at work and (open) _____ the case.
                      10   **11**

I (have) _____ the man's briefcase! While I (look) _____
              12   **13**

in the briefcase, my phone (ring) _____ . The man from the bus
                                    14

(tell) _____ me that he (have) _____ my case. He
              15   **16**

(tell) _____ me that his name was Lee. We (decide) _____
              17   **18**

to meet after work.

E. A: What (do) _____ you _____ Saturday night?
                              1   (1)

   B: Not much. I (watch) _____ a DVD when my old roommate
                                      2

       from college (call) _____. She lives in Washington D.C. now. We
                                    3

       (talk) _____ for an hour. How about you?
                       4

    A: Well, I (wait) _____ for my friend at a movie, but she
                          5

       (not, come) _____!
                      6

    B: What (do) _____ you _____?
                       7   (7)

    A: When I (call) _____ her, she (wait) _____
                       8   9

       for a taxi. She finally (arrive) _____ after the movie. We
                                      10

       (have) _____ coffee and (talk) _____.
                  11   12

F. We (walk) _____ to school when we (see) _____
                    1   2

the accident. A car (go) _____ very fast when it (hit)
                                3

_____ a bicycle rider. We (call) _____ 911, and an
            4   5

ambulance and the police (come) _____. While the police (talk)
                                6

_____ to the driver, the driver (be) _____ very
           7   8

upset and nervous. The driver (say) _____ he (not, see) _____
                               9   10

the bicycle. Fortunately, the bicycle rider (wear) _____ a helmet.
                                             11

G. A: (like) _____ you _____ the movie?
                                 1   (1)

  B: It (be) _____ okay. The man behind me (talk) _____ for
                      2   3

    a long time while I (watch) _____ the film. I (turn) _____
                                        4   5

    and (ask) _____ him to be quiet. He (get) _____ angry
                       6   7

    and (start) _____ talking more!
                          8

8   Practice

Write *C* next to the sentence if the simple past or past progressive is used correctly. Write *I* if the simple past or past progressive is used incorrectly.

    I   **1.** While I saw him, I smiled.

  _____ **2.** She took a shower when she got home.

  _____ **3.** The phone rang while I was making dinner.

  _____ **4.** While I heard the music, I closed my eyes.

  _____ **5.** When she was arriving, I picked her up at the airport.

  _____ **6.** While Mr. Jones was teaching, the students listened carefully.

9   Practice

Read the following sentences. Decide which action happened or was in progress first. Circle the letter *a* or *b*.

1. I smiled when I saw her.
    a. First I saw her, then I smiled.
    b. I was smiling before I saw her.

2. I was smiling when I saw her.
    a. First I saw her, then I smiled.
    b. I was smiling before I saw her.

3. Becky was doing her homework when her computer crashed.
   a. First the computer crashed, then she did her homework.
   b. She started her homework before the computer crashed.

4. We knew something was wrong when we saw him.
   a. First we saw him, then we knew something was wrong.
   b. We knew something was wrong before we saw him.

5. When Joe asked a question, the teacher was talking.
   a. First Joe asked a question, then the teacher said something.
   b. The teacher started talking before Joe asked his question.

6. When Cheryl got up, she looked out the window.
   a. First Cheryl got up, then she looked out the window.
   b. She started looking out the window before she got up.

7. I wasn't wearing a hat when it started to rain.
   a. First it started to rain, then I didn't have a hat.
   b. I didn't have a hat before it started to rain.

8. Maria made tea while her husband was sleeping.
   a. First Maria made tea, then her husband slept.
   b. Her husband started to sleep before she made her tea.

9. When the package didn't arrive, Danny called the company.
   a. First the package didn't arrive, then Danny called the company.
   b. Danny called the company before he knew the package didn't arrive.

10. Everyone clapped when the concert finished.
    a. First the concert finished, then the people clapped.
    b. The people started clapping before the end of the concert.

11. When they finished dinner, they washed the dishes.
    a. First they finished dinner, then they washed the dishes.
    b. They started washing the dishes before they finished dinner.

12. We saw them while they were eating the snacks.
    a. First we saw them, then they ate the snacks.
    b. They started eating the snacks before we saw them.

10 Practice

Look at the following results of different actions. Write what you think the person was doing in each situation. Use *while* or *when* in your sentences.

1. She started to smile.

   When she looked at the babies, she started to smile .

2. Jason had an accident.

   _____ .

3. He cooked a big dinner.

_____.

4. The police came.

_____.

5. His mother laughed.

_____.

6. I heard footsteps in the house.

_____.

7. The children started crying.

_____.

8. We didn't go to school.

_____.

9. Lily didn't send the letter.

_____.

10. I didn't take her photo.

_____.

II Practice

Use your own experiences to complete the sentences.

1. When I heard the news, ____*I was surprised and started laughing*____.

2. _____ when I saw her/him for the first time.

3. I turned off the TV when _____.

4. While I was coming home yesterday, _____.

5. While I was sleeping last night, _____.

6. _____ when _____.

7. While _____, _____.

8. When _____, _____.

9. _____ while _____.

SELF-TEST

A **Choose the best answer, A, B, C, or D, to complete the sentence. Mark your answer by darkening the oval with the same letter.**

1. I came into the room while _____.

   A. they dancing (A) (B) (C) (D)
   B. they were dancing
   C. danced
   D. are dancing

2. Andy _____ the car when you called.

   A. was fixing (A) (B) (C) (D)
   B. fix
   C. am fixing
   D. were fixing

3. At 6:00 last night, I _____.

   A. didn't making dinner (A) (B) (C) (D)
   B. making dinner
   C. am making dinner
   D. was making dinner

4. His father _____ the newspaper every morning.

   A. wasn't read (A) (B) (C) (D)
   B. is reading
   C. reads
   D. read

5. We _____ to the store yesterday.

   A. didn't go (A) (B) (C) (D)
   B. wasn't go
   C. isn't going
   D. go

6. _____ I got up, it was raining.

   A. While (A) (B) (C) (D)
   B. When
   C. Last
   D. Ago

7. Denny _____ when the teacher asked him a question.

   A. isn't listening (A) (B) (C) (D)
   B. listen
   C. didn't listening
   D. wasn't listening

8. Yoko was carrying a heavy box when she _____.

   A. fall (A) (B) (C) (D)
   B. fell
   C. isn't falling
   D. falls

9. Look! _____ that girl across the street?

   A. See you (A) (B) (C) (D)
   B. Are you seeing
   C. Do you see
   D. Were you seeing

10. What _____ at midnight last night?

    A. did you (A) (B) (C) (D)
    B. are you doing
    C. were you do
    D. were you doing

B **Find the underlined word or phrase, A, B, C, or D, that is incorrect. Mark your answer by darkening the oval with the same letter.**

1. While the people were watched the show
   A   B
   last night, I fell asleep.
   C   D

   Ⓐ Ⓑ Ⓒ Ⓓ

2. Those girls were talking when the
   A   B   C
   earthquake happen.
              D

   Ⓐ Ⓑ Ⓒ Ⓓ

3. She was thinking about her boyfriend
   A   B
   when she was saw him at the corner.
   C   D

   Ⓐ Ⓑ Ⓒ Ⓓ

4. They not had a good time while they were
        A   B   C
   on vacation last year.
              D

   Ⓐ Ⓑ Ⓒ Ⓓ

5. He didn't answered the phone when
      A   C
   I called him.
      D

   Ⓐ Ⓑ Ⓒ Ⓓ

6. Dorothy laughed when she was hearing
           A   B   C
   the funny story.
       D

   Ⓐ Ⓑ Ⓒ Ⓓ

7. My family was watching TV when we feel
   A   B   C   D
   the earthquake.

   Ⓐ Ⓑ Ⓒ Ⓓ

8. They wasn't looking when Gerald took
        A   B   C
   their picture.
       D

   Ⓐ Ⓑ Ⓒ Ⓓ

9. While the people were sleeping, the fire
   A   B   C
   start.
   D

   Ⓐ Ⓑ Ⓒ Ⓓ

10. Yesterday, when Rachel was walked to
    A   B   C
    school, she saw her best friend.
                D

    Ⓐ Ⓑ Ⓒ Ⓓ